Edible Flowers

DESSERTS & DRINKS

CATHY WILKINSON BARASH

FULCRUM PUBLISHING

To Fritz and May, who all those years ago told me not *to eat the flowers.*

Library of Congress Cataloging-in-Publication Data

Barash, Cathy Wilkinson.
   Edible flowers : desserts and drinks / Cathy Wilkinson Barash.
      p.   cm.
   Includes index.
   ISBN 1-55591-389-X (pbk.)
   1. Cookery (Flowers) 2. Flower gardening. 3. Flowers.
I. Title.
TX814.5.F5B365   1997
641.6'59—dc21
                                              97-11851
                                              CIP

Printed in Korea
0 9 8 7 6 5 4 3 2 1

Fulcrum Publishing
350 Indiana Street, Suite 350
Golden, Colorado 80401-5093
(800) 992-2908 • (303) 277-1623

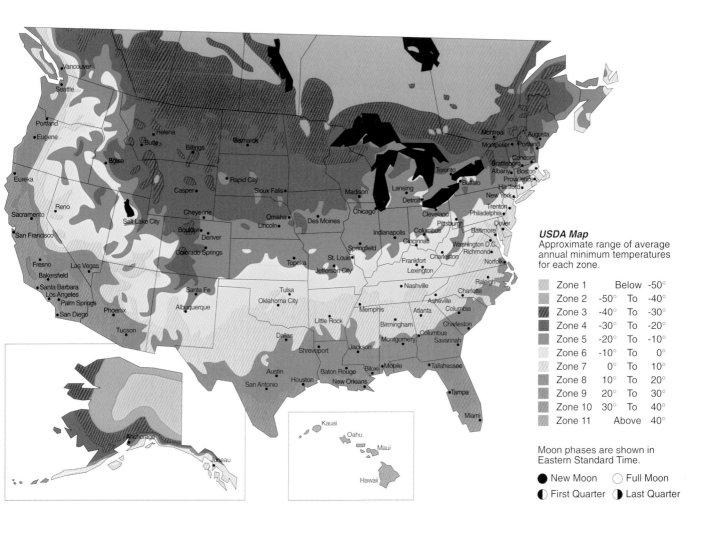

USDA Map
Approximate range of average annual minimum temperatures for each zone.

	Zone 1	Below	-50°
	Zone 2	-50° To	-40°
	Zone 3	-40° To	-30°
	Zone 4	-30° To	-20°
	Zone 5	-20° To	-10°
	Zone 6	-10° To	0°
	Zone 7	0° To	10°
	Zone 8	10° To	20°
	Zone 9	20° To	30°
	Zone 10	30° To	40°
	Zone 11	Above	40°

Moon phases are shown in Eastern Standard Time.

● New Moon   ○ Full Moon
◐ First Quarter   ◑ Last Quarter

CONTENTS

ACKNOWLEDGMENTS

So many people were helpful in creating this book. I could never have done it without so much generous help and support. My heartfelt thanks go to:

The Inspiration

All who have been involved in this project from its inception, saw its potential, and whose enthusiasm kept me and this book going—Mary Moss, Toodie Walt, Lynne Shaner, Sam Barash, Barbara Wilkinson and my agent Kit Ward. Jay Staten, Alison Auch and Alyssa Pumphrey at Fulcrum.

The Plant People—Green Thumbs Up

The people who are on the cutting edge with edible flowers, those who grew gardens for me and the friends who let me run amok in their gardens, pillaging and photographing—Ros Creasy; Sinclair Philip and Byron Cook at Sooke Harbour House; Carole Saville; Fetzer Vineyards; Joe Queriolo at Mudd's Restaurant; Katarina Eriksson at the Parkway Grill; Eileen and Fred Mendyka at Good Thyme Farm; Warren Leach and Philip Boucher at Tranquil Lake Nursery; Pat Lanza; Renee Sheperd; Liz Ball; Toodie Walt; Franny Elder; Craig Zaffee and Tricia Sweeney; Susan and Jay Kuhlman; Donna and Andy Durbridge.

The Food People

All the chefs, cooks and gardeners whose creative recipes grace these pages. Food tasters—Dency Kane, Donna and Andy Durbridge, Rizz and Tucker Dean, Janine Adams, "Annie Hyssop" Arthur.

Technical Support

Ethnobotanists—Dr. James Duke and Dr. Nancy Turner for their expertise in checking the flowers for edibility, safety and especially for keeping cautious. Photographic technology—the folks at Jomark. General assistance—Elisa Robinson. Moral support and sharing her abundant knowledge—Ros Creasy.

The Other Helpful Folks

Sally Ferguson of Netherlands FlowerBulb Information Center; Felder Rushing, for keeping the fun in it all; Bob at MMA Earthly Delights who can always find edible flowers, even in winter; Sinclair Philip of Sooke Harbour House, which is for me the mecca of edible flowers both in the garden and kitchen.

The Home Front

Those who kept things going while I was on the road photographing and gathering recipes, and while I was home—my landlady and good friend, Rizz Arthur Dean, who let me grow edible flowers throughout the property; and especially my cat Sebastian. And my dear friend, David Wierdsma, who has captured the goddess within me.

*I*NTRODUCTION

Have you ever eaten a flower? Think before you answer. You may have enjoyed edible flowers without realizing it. Do you like artichokes? They are immature flowers; although you may argue that technically speaking, you haven't eaten flowers, only buds.

When was the last time you had Chinese hot and sour soup? Dried daylily petals are a key ingredient. Have you had a cup of refreshing herbal tea lately? Look at the box on your kitchen shelf. The ingredients may include rose petals, hibiscus, mint, chamomile or other familiar flowers.

As much as I enjoy edible flowers, I rarely graze through a flower border. Take a moment before you rush outside to your own garden to consider how to get the most out of your edible flower experience.

FLOWERS FOR THE PALATE— FRESH AND PRESERVED

It is more important to collect flowers for eating at the optimum time than those going into an arrangement. Pick flowers in the cool of the day, preferably in early morning after the dew has evaporated. Choose flowers that are at their peak. Flowers that are not fully open, those that are past their prime and flowers that are starting to wilt should be passed. Think of

flowers as fruit. Unripe fruit or flowers do not have the superb flavor of those at the height of ripeness, while those that are overripe also pall by comparison with those at peak development.

After picking, put those with long stems into water. Keep them cool, flowers are perishable and will wilt in a warm place. Pick short-stemmed blooms within three or four hours of using and put them between layers of damp paper toweling or in a plastic bag in the refrigerator. Immediately before using, gently wash the flowers, checking carefully for bugs and dirt. Before washing all the flowers, do a test on one flower. Some are fragile and water will discolor them. Such flowers need an extra careful insect inspection.

THE PROOF IS IN THE TASTING

Always sample a flower before using it for cooking. Obviously, if a recipe calls for a cup of lavender flowers, don't taste each flower. Taste one as representative. If you are picking lavender from two different areas in the garden or from two different varieties, sample one of each. Do the tasting before beginning picking. In that way, if for some reason the flower tastes terrible, no time or energy is wasted on picking flowers that won't be used.

When tasting an edible flower, especially for the first time (even if it is something that has been growing in the garden for years, do it at least once a season), I use a technique somewhat similar to wine-tasting that I am happy to share with you. Choose a flower at its peak of perfection. Examine it, looking for lurking insects which might badly affect the taste test. Remove the pistils and stamen. If at any point during this process you find that the flower is disagreeable or objectionable in any way—spit it out (discreetly, of course). There is

nothing that says that you have to like every flower. Soil and growing conditions can affect the flavor. Some flowers have so many different hybrids or cultivated varieties (cultivars) that there are bound to be one or two that don't suit your taste.

Smell the flower. If it smells good, continue. Take a tiny bite of the flower. Relax and close your eyes so that all your attention is focused on the sensations you are getting from the flower. Chew it carefully with your front teeth. Breathe in through your mouth to get the essence of the flower. After chewing the flower, slowly roll it over your tongue, allowing the taste buds to sense the different components that make up a flavor—bitter, sweet, sour, salty. Finally swallow the flower.

WHAT PART OF THE FLOWER TO EAT

Remove the stamens and styles from flowers before eating. The pollen can detract from the flavor of the flower. In addition, the pollen may cause an allergic reaction in susceptible individuals. Remove the sepals of all flowers except violas, Johnny-jump-ups and pansies.

Only the petals of some flowers such as rose, calendula, tulip, chrysanthemum, yucca and lavender are edible. When using just the petals, separate them from the rest of the flower just prior to use to keep wilting to a minimum. Others, including Johnny-jump-up, violet, runner bean, honeysuckle and clover can be eaten in their entirety.

Roses, dianthus, English daisies, marigolds and chrysanthemums have a bitter white portion at the base of the petal where it was attached to the flower. Break or cut off the bitter part off the petal before using.

PRESERVING FLOWERS

In the scheme of things, plants are trying to reproduce themselves. The flower is the first step in that process. In simplistic terms, after the flower is fertilized, a seed is set and the plant can die happy, knowing it has furthered its species. If, however, the flower is picked (or even better all the flowers are picked), the process is disrupted and the plant has to start all over again, by putting out additional flowers. Thus with many, but alas not all, plants you can extend the bloom period by harvesting flowers before they set seed.

For me the edible flowers go by in my garden too quickly. It is nice to be able to extend the enjoyment of the flowers past the weeks or months they are available fresh from the garden. There are several ways to preserve flowers for days, weeks or months. Each has it advantages and disadvantages and may not work for all flowers. Freezing, which is the best way of preserving vegetables, unfortunately, does not work for most flowers (daylilies are an exception); they are too fragile. However, flowers or petals can be successfully frozen in ice cubes to enliven a drink any time of year. Drying works well for some, yet flavor is somewhat altered. Candying is time-consuming, but will preserve sweet flowers and petals for a long time. Flowers can also be preserved by making flower butter, sugar, oil, vinegar, syrup, etc. Flower butter changes the flavor the least.

DRYING

Gather flowers early in the day before the sun shines on them. Hang by the stems in a warm, dark area with good air circulation. Individual flowers can be dried differently. Place the clean flowers in a single layer on fine mesh. Let them dry in a warm, dark, dust-free area.

Once flowers are dry, store them whole, crumbled or pulverized (sieved) in airtight glass containers in a cool, dark place. In recipes calling for fresh flowers, substitute half the amount if using dried.

OTHER PRESERVATION METHODS

FLOWER JELLY

—

from Libby Goldstein, Philadelphia, Pennsylvania

1 cup solidly packed flowers (1 or more types according to taste)
1-1/4 cups water
1/2 cup herb or flower vinegar
3-1/2 cups granulated sugar
1 pouch liquid pectin

Steep the flowers in the water in a covered glass or ceramic container for 1 to 2 days or until the liquid smells and tastes of the flowers.

Strain the infusion into a 6-quart nonreactive Dutch oven or preserving pan. Add vinegar and then the sugar and let it dissolve without stirring. When the sugar has dissolved, put the pot over a high heat and, stirring all the while, bring to a full rolling boil. Add the pectin. Return to boil for 1 minute or as long as package directions suggest. Remove from heat and skim off any foam.

Ladle jelly into 3 or 4 hot, sterilized half-pint jars, leaving 1/8-inch head space. Wipe the jar rims with a hot damp cloth, screw on canning lids that have been prepared according to manufacturer's directions and tighten. Process for 5 minutes in a boiling water bath; turn upside down for 5 minutes to make sure the lids seal.

An alternative is to boil the water and pour it over the flowers in a glass or stoneware container. Let steep, covered for 10 to 15 minutes. The cold water method usually results in a clearer jelly.

These jellies make excellent glazes for roast or broiled poultry and pork. Some are good on fish, carrots or sweet potatoes. They are also tasty toppings to open-face tea sandwiches

Makes 3 to 4-1/2 pints.

EDIBLE FLOWERS

FLOWER BUTTER

1/2 cup flowers
1/2 pound sweet (unsalted) butter

Finely chop flower petals and mix into softened butter. Put in a glass bowl and cover with plastic wrap.
Let the mix sit at room temperature for several hours, then refrigerate for several days to bring out the flavor.

Flower butter may be kept refrigerated for 2 weeks or frozen for up to 6 months.

Almost all edible flowers may be mixed in with butter. Of course the flavors will vary with the flowers.

Spread butter on bread or make your favorite sugar cookie or pound cake, substituting flower butter for regular butter.

FLOWER HONEY

1/2 to 1 cup chopped fresh flower petals or crushed dried petals
1 pound honey

Add flowers to a jar of honey. Cover the jar loosely and place in a pan half full of gently boiling water. Remove from heat and let sit in the hot water for 10 minutes. Remove the jar from the water and allow to cool to room temperature.

Tighten the cover. Let it sit for at least 1 week. If desired, strain before eating.

To preserve the flavor of good quality, never heat it to more than 140°F.

Makes about 2 cups honey.

FLOWER SUGAR

2 cups granulated sugar
1/2 to 1 cup minced flower petals (a sweet flavor is preferable)

Pound sugar and minced flower petals in a mortar, or process them well in a food processor. Put into a clean glass jar,

cover and let stand 1 week. Sift, if desired, and store in an airtight container. Flower sugar is an elegant topping, lightly sprinkled over a fruit sorbet.

Makes about 2-1/2 cups sugar.

FLOWER SYRUP

1 cup water
3 cups granulated sugar
1/2 to 1 cup flower petals, whole or chopped

Boil all ingredients for 10 minutes, or until thickened into a syrup. Strain through cheesecloth into a clean glass jar. Seal and store in the refrigerator for up to 2 weeks.

Use as a base for making sorbet or pudding. Pour over fruit. Delicious on pancakes.

Makes about 2 to 3 cups syrup.

CANDIED FLOWERS

1 egg white
100-proof vodka
superfine granulated sugar
thin artist's paintbrush
violets (or other flower to be candied—pansy, Johnny-jump-up, rose petals, lilac, borage, pea, pinks, scented geranium)
wire cake rack
baking parchment

In small bowl, beat the egg whites to a light froth. Add 1 or 2 drops of vodka and mix. This helps the flower to dry quicker. Pour sugar into a shallow bowl. Have the paintbrush at hand and some freshly picked violets. I find it best to pick no more than 4 or 5 at a time, candy them and then pick more. Even with putting them in water, they wilt quickly, making the process more difficult. Cover a wire cake rack with baking parchment. Now you are ready to start.

Grasp the top of the stem of a violet between thumb and forefinger. Dip the paintbrush in the beaten egg white. Gently paint all surfaces of the petals of the flower with the egg white. Make sure to get between all petals. Gently sprinkle the sugar on the flower, making sure to cover all surfaces and between the petals. Place the flower face up on the parchment. Repeat process with another flower.

Do not be discouraged—this is a slow process that requires meticulous attention to detail. When you have done as many flowers as to fill the parchment, place them (still on the rack) in a cool, dry, well-ventilated area to allow to dry completely. When the flowers dry, they will be stiff and brittle. Store in an airtight container.

If you live in a very humid area, it can complicate matters. You may dry the flowers in a room with a dehumidifier. Once dry, gently place them in a heavy-duty plastic freezer container, layered no more than 3 deep, separated by a sheet of parchment. Keep them in the freezer up to a year. If you store them at room temperature, the humidity creeps in and they can turn into green mush after a couple of months.

EDIBLE FLOWERS

FLOWER VODKA

2 cups good quality vodka
1/4 to 1/2 cup flower petals

Add flowers to the vodka. Let sit at least 48 hours at room temperature. Strain the vodka. Pour into attractive bottles and store in the freezer. Serve in small thimble-sized glasses.

The best flowers to add to vodka are tuberous begonias (what a great color it turns!), clove pinks, orange, lemon and rose, but experiment with other flowers as well. Drink this straight for best enjoyment.

Makes about 2 cups vodka.

FRITTER BATTER

1 cup unbleached flour
1/4 teaspoon salt
1 tablespoon sugar
2 eggs, separated
1 tablespoon melted butter
2/3 cup milk
1 cup flower petals
1 tablespoon peanut oil (or more if needed)
confectioners' sugar

Mix the flour, salt and sugar. In a separate bowl, beat the egg yolks with the melted butter. Slowly add the flour to the egg

yolk mixture. Once that is mixed, gradually beat in the milk. Beat the egg whites until stiff. Fold them into the batter just before cooking. Gently fold in flower petals.

Heat a skillet. Add enough peanut oil to lightly coat the bottom. Drop the batter by rounded tablespoonful into the hot skillet and fry to a golden brown. When bubbles on top of fritters break, turn fritters over and brown second side. Serve immediately, sprinkled with confectioners' sugar. These are best fresh, but frozen fritters keep well up to 3 months.

Serves 4 to 6.

The Ten Rules of Edible Flowers

1. Eat flowers only when you are positive they are edible.

2. Just because it is served with food does not mean a flower is edible (see Rule 1).

3. Eat only flowers that have been grown organically.

4. Do not eat flowers from florists, nurseries or garden centers (see Rule 3).

5. If you have hay fever, asthma or allergies, do not eat flowers.

6. Do not eat flowers picked from the side of the road. They are contaminated from car emissions (see Rule 3).

7. Remove pistils and stamens from flowers before eating. Eat only the petals.

8. Not all flowers are edible. Some are poisonous.

9. There are many varieties of any one flower. Flowers taste different when grown in different locations.

10. Introduce flowers into your diet the way you would new foods to a baby—one at a time in small quantities.

ANISE HYSSOP

ANISE HYSSOP
Agastache foeniculum
(A. anethiodora)
Mint family
Lamiaceae
Anise flavor
Perennial (Zones 8–10)
Any well-drained soil
Full sun to light shade

Anise hyssop is a tender perennial that grows three to four feet tall. Like other members of the mint family, the stems are square. The three- to four-inch ovate leaves have serrated edges. They appear opposite on the stems.

The upright branching plant has dense, deep lilac-colored, terminal flower spikes five to six inches long that begin to bloom in midsummer. Look closely at the spikes and you can see the small, two-lipped flowers. As the flowers fade from the spikes, cut the spikes down to the nearest leafing branches. You will be rewarded with more flowers later in the season, although the spikes will not be as showy as the earlier ones. The flowers produce abundant nectar that yields a light, fragrant honey.

The entire plant has a lovely anise scent to it, indicative of the flavor of both the flowers and the leaves. Although anise hyssop is not one of the best known herbs, the flavor of the flowers is wonderful. When I eat an anise hyssop flower, I am carried back to the days of my childhood, at a thirty-five-cent Saturday movie matinee, eating Good 'n' Plenty candies.

CULTURE

Anise hyssop prefers full sun, but will grow in light shade in any well-drained soil.

It grows easily from seed. Plant outdoors as soon as all danger of frost is past, or sow seeds indoors at least six weeks before the last frost. Transplant outdoors, allowing at least twelve to fifteen inches between plants. Unlike many perennials started from seed, anise hyssop will flower the first summer. You can sow anise hyssop directly in the garden in the fall in warm climates.

Anise hyssop dies back to the ground after a killing frost. Anise hyssop is late to come up in the spring. The second year I had it, I despaired of it coming back and purchased four new plants. I stuck them in the garden and then saw the tiny emerging leaves of my one-year-old plants. Never one to waste anything, I dug them up and shared them with friends. Soon I saw many others coming up nearby; anise hyssop does self-seed.

ANISE HYSSOP FLOWER CUSTARD WITH BLACK PANSY SYRUP

from David Feys, co-chef, Sooke Harbour House, Sooke, British Columbia, Canada

Custard:

1 cup whole milk

1 cup whipping cream

1/4 cup granulated sugar

6 tablespoons anise hyssop flowers

2 large eggs

3 large egg yolks

Garnish:

2 cups Black Pansy Syrup (see page 45)

6 teaspoons anise hyssop flowers

6 anise hyssop leaves

6 black pansy flowers

Combine milk and cream. Pour half of this mixture into a small saucepan with the sugar and the anise hyssop flowers. Scald the mixture over a low heat. Remove from heat and add remaining milk mixture. Stir well and set aside to cool. Cover and refrigerate overnight, if possible. The length of time allotted to let the anise hyssop steep in this mixture will greatly affect the finished product.

Preheat oven to 350°F. Prepare a 9-by-13-inch Pyrex or aluminum pan with enough hot water to reach halfway up the sides of custard molds. Put this prepared bain marie into the oven.

In a medium-sized bowl, beat the eggs and egg yolks well. Add the cooled infused milk mixture. Combine well and pour equal amounts into 6 clean, dry custard molds.

Bake custard in the bain marie for 25 to 30 minutes. To test for doneness, insert a small knife into the center of a custard. If clean when removed, it is properly cooked. Use a pair of tongs to remove custard molds from the bain marie to a cooling rack. Allow to cool completely. Refrigerate for at least 1 hour.

Remove the custard by running a small knife around the edge of the mold and inverting directly onto a serving plate. Pour the syrup over the top of the custard. Decorate each plate with 1 teaspoon anise hyssop flowers, 1 anise hyssop leaf and black pansy flower.

Serves 6.

ANISE HYSSOP BUTTER COOKIES

1 cup all-purpose flour

1/4 cup plus 2 tablespoons confectioners' sugar

pinch of salt

7 ounces sweet (unsalted) butter, cold and cut into small pieces

1 teaspoon vanilla

2 tablespoons anise hyssop flowers, minced

Fit a food processor with the plastic blade. Add flour, sugar and salt. Add the butter and process until ingredients are just combined, about 2 minutes. Add vanilla and anise hyssop flowers, processing for an additional 2 minutes. Remove the dough from the processor and shape it into a ball. Roll it into a 1-inch thick log and wrap it with waxed paper. Refrigerate for 1 hour.

Preheat oven to 375°F. Unwrap log and slice it into 1/4-inch rounds. Place cookies on a ungreased cookie sheet. Bake for 7 to 10 minutes, or until lightly golden. Delicious right from the oven.

Makes 36 cookies.

APPLE

The botanic name for apple is derived from the Latin *malum*, meaning apple. Most modern apples are descended from *Malus pumila*, which was the original apple. Apples are among the oldest of all cultivated fruits. They are known to have been in cultivation since prehistoric times. The first written record of the apple is in the book of Genesis in the Bible. Despite being the temptation that drove man out of Eden, apples have continued to enjoy popularity throughout the millennia.

The pharaohs grew apples along the Nile in Egypt more than three thousand years ago. In ancient Greece apples were a rare commodity. A bride and groom, by law, could share one apple between them on their wedding day. In the Victorian language of flowers, apple means preference.

The modern apple is native to the Caucasus Mountains of western Asia. Like many of the herbs, it was brought to England by the Romans in the third and fourth centuries. Apples were first brought to the New World in 1623 by William Blackstone, an Episcopal priest. No one has done more to popularize apples than Jonathan Chapman (a.k.a. Johnny Appleseed). He was known as a missionary nurseryman who gave away apple seeds to everyone he met as he journeyed from Pennsylvania to Illinois.

Apples are generally rounded trees that can grow to fifty feet tall, but are usually much smaller, especially in cultivation, where the average height is twenty to twenty-

APPLE
Malus spp.
Rose family
Rosaceae
Floral flavor
Tree (Zones 3–10)
Deep, fertile soil
Full sun

five feet. Dwarf (up to six feet tall) and semi-dwarf trees (up to fifteen feet) are regular trees grafted onto dwarfing stock. Genetic dwarfs are the smallest of all fruit trees. Recently introduced, they are dwarf as a result of breeding, not grafting. For the home garden, these are more practical.

The trees are attractive with elliptical, leathery leaves with serrated edges. The leaves are a smooth bright green above while paler underneath. Flowers appear in early spring at about the same time the leaves emerge. The flowers are about two inches across with five petals that are white flushed with pink. Flowers grow in groups of three to six at the tips of young leaves. Although a lone apple tree will flower, two or three compatible varieties (that bloom at the same time) must be planted for cross-pollination and resulting fruiting. If the flower is pollinated, the fruit will grow, ripening in late summer or fall, depending on the variety.

The flowers have a mildly sweet, floral flavor. They are a nice accompaniment to fruit dishes and can easily be candied to use as garnish later in the season.

CULTURE

Apples must grow in full sun for good flowering and fruit production. They prefer deep, fertile, moist, well-drained soil.

Check with your local Cooperative Extension Service to find the apple varieties that are best suited for growing in your area. Plant the trees only when they are dormant, in early spring for zones 3 to 7, and in fall for zones 8 to 10. Allow twenty feet between standard trees, twelve feet between semi-dwarf varieties and eight feet between dwarf trees. Genetic dwarfs are suitable for planting in containers that are at least two to two and one-half feet in diameter.

Do not fertilize at the time of planting; it can burn the roots. Add two to four inches of light organic mulch around the base of the tree. Do not mulch right up to the trunk of the tree.

WARNING

Apple flowers should be eaten in moderation as they may contain cyanide precursors.

STRAWBERRIES AND KIWI WITH APPLE BLOSSOMS

1 pint strawberries, cleaned, stemmed and cut in half
2 kiwis, peeled and sliced
apple petals

Place kiwi around the sides of individual glass dessert bowls. Add strawberry halves in the center. Top with apple petals.

An elegant-looking dessert that is quick and easy to make. For added richness, serve with a dollop of Sweet Woodruff Yogurt Custard (see page 67).

Serves 4.

BEE BALM

Bee balm is so named as evidence of bee's love for the flower's nectar. Oswego Indians made a tea from bee balm, which they shared with the American colonists. After the Boston Tea Party, bee balm tea was the beverage of choice. Even today it is still popular. Bee balm is also known as Oswego tea, named for the Indian tribe who, like the Shakers, favored it above others. The name bergamot comes from the similarity between the fragrance of bee balm and that of the bergamot orange.

Bee balm distinguishes itself as one of the few native American herbs. It grows wild in moist woods, thickets along stream banks from Michigan to New York and south to Tennessee and Georgia, especially in upland areas. A distinctive perennial herb, bee balm grows two to three feet tall with a large ragged head of bright crimson flowers and reddish bracts from late June to September. Like other members of the mint family, it has square stems and opposite leaves. The brilliant flowers make this a good choice to plant in a perennial border.

The flavor can be described as citrusy, sweet, hot and minty.

Monarda fistulosa, wild bergamot, is distinguished by its pinkish or pale lavender flowers with lilac tinged bracts. Its flavor can be quite intense, spicy and minty at the same time. It is commonly used in the Pacific Northwest as a spicy garnish to salads or vegetables.

CULTURE

Bee balm grows best in partial shade or full sun in rich, moist soil.

BEE BALM (Oswego tea, red bergamot)
Monarda didyma
Mint family
Lamiaceae
Mint flavor
Perennial (Zones 4–8)
Moist, rich soil
Partial shade to full sun

Start the seed in a cold frame in midsummer. By the following spring it will be strong enough to be transplanted. An alternative is to direct seed bee balm into the garden in November. The seeds will germinate in the spring. By the second year it will reach its mature size.

Bee balm can be propagated from root divisions. It usually needs dividing about every three years. Dig up the fibrous roots in early spring. Divide and replant the outer roots, which are the newer roots, and discard the center. Allow at least eighteen inches between plants.

To get the largest blooms, the plant should not be allowed to flower the first year. Cut back any flower heads as they form. The second and subsequent years, cut the flower head back after it blooms, and you may be rewarded with a second flowering in the fall.

After a killing frost, cut back the stalks almost to ground level and mulch the plant well. In spring, remember to remove the mulch.

BEE BALM ICE CREAM

1 cup milk

1-inch length vanilla bean

2 tablespoons red bee balm flowers, cut into 1/4-inch lengths

1/4 cup granulated sugar

1-1/2 cups cream

3 egg yolks

sugar, stir and heat slowly until mixture is hot. Do not let it boil. Add cream, heat until mixture is hot, not to a boil.

Beat egg yolks until frothy. Mix a small amount of the hot liquid into the beaten yolks, then pour the warmed yolks into the milk. Continue to stir over a low heat until liquid thickens and coats a wooden spoon.

Remove from heat and let cool to room temperature. Remove vanilla bean. Process in an ice cream maker according to manufacturer's directions. This ice cream has a surprisingly nutty flavor. It takes a bit of time to make, but is well worth the effort.

Serves 4 to 6.

Pour milk into a heavy saucepan and place over a low heat. Add vanilla and flowers; stir until milk is lukewarm. Add

BEE BALM POUND CAKE

1 cup butter

2 cups granulated sugar

2-1/4 cups all-purpose flour

6 eggs

juice of 1 lemon

1 teaspoon vanilla

1/2 cup bee balm flowers, coarsely chopped

1/8 teaspoon salt

Preheat oven to 325°F. Cream together butter and sugar until mixture is light and fluffy.

In a separate bowl, sift and then measure flour. Alternate adding flour and eggs (one at a time) to the creamed sugar, beating continually. Add lemon juice, vanilla, bee balm flowers and salt. Mix for 1 minute.

Pour batter into a buttered and floured tube pan and bake for about 1 hour and 20 minutes, or until a toothpick inserted in the center comes out clean. Take cake out of the oven and put on a rack to cool for 10 minutes. Remove cake from pan and allow to cool completely on rack.

Serves 15 to 20.

BEE BALM TEA

2 tablespoons bee balm flowers, chopped

4 cups water, boiling

Steep flowers in water for 5 to 10 minutes. Strain and serve.

Serves 4.

BEE BALM TARTLETS

Filling:

1 cup freshly squeezed lemon juice

1 cup granulated sugar

3 eggs

3 egg yolks

10 tablespoons butter, cut into small pieces

1/4 cup bee balm flowers, coarsely chopped

In the top of a double boiler, mix lemon juice and sugar. Heat until the sugar is dissolved, stirring occasionally with a wooden spoon. Add eggs and egg yolks, stirring continually for about 10 minutes until the mixture thickens and coats the back of the spoon. Add butter, stirring until completely combined. Stir in bee balm. Remove from heat, transfer to a glass or stainless steel bowl and refrigerate overnight or until set.

Tartlets:

6 tablespoons butter, softened and cut into small pieces

5 tablespoons granulated sugar

2 tablespoons water

1 egg

1 egg yolk

2 cups all-purpose flour

flour for dusting board

Fit a food processor with the plastic blade. Add butter and sugar; cream together. Add water, egg and egg yolk. Process until just mixed. Add flour, processing until well mixed. Remove dough from processor bowl. Divide dough in half, wrap each half in waxed paper and refrigerate for at least 2 hours.

Remove dough from refrigerator. Dust a wooden board with flour. One at a time, roll the dough halves out to a thickness of 1/8 inch. Cut with a 3- to 4-inch cookie cutter (use a glass if you don't have a cutter). Fit each piece of cut dough into 2-inch tartlet pans or miniature muffin tins. This should make 24 tartlets. Prick the bottom of each with a fork and refrigerate for 1 hour.

Preheat oven to 375°F. Remove tart pans from refrigerator and bake on a cookie sheet for 7 to 8 minutes, or until they just turn golden. Remove from oven and set aside to cool.

Just before serving, spoon filling into cooled tartlet shells. Garnish with additional flowers.

Makes 24 tartlets.

BORAGE

BORAGE
(Bee bread, Starflower, Common bugloss)
Borago officinalis
Borage family
Boraginaceae
Herbal flavor
Annual, self-seeding
Light, poor, dry soil
Full sun

The word borage is likely a derivation from the Latin *burra* meaning a shaggy garment, referring to the rough foliage of this lovely herb. Borage was once believed to have great powers. According to Pliny it brought happiness and joy where it grew. In Gerard's *Herball*, he quotes the belief that had been carried down from the ancient Greeks and Romans, "I, borage, bring always courage." In the Victorian language of flowers, borage means bluntness.

Borage is an annual herb with dark gray-green, hairy leaves with a cucumber flavor. Borage is native to the Mediterranean area. Cultivated in northern Europe, it was brought by settlers to America. It was purportedly planted by Columbus' men on Isabella's Island. It was first listed in an American seed catalog in 1806. In the past, it was grown more as a medicinal than a culinary herb, but now its subtle flavor is becoming more appreciated.

Borage grows eighteen to twenty-four inches, but I have seen it up to four feet tall in California, with prickly hairs covering virtually the entire plant. The leaves are large and oval with wavy edges, growing alternately along hollow, somewhat succulent, branched stems. The small (one inch) star-shaped, brilliant blue (rarely rose) flowers, borne in clusters from April to November (depending on the area of the country) are very attractive to bees. In midsummer a plant may seem to be abuzz with all the activity.

The flavor of borage, both petals and leaves, is mildly like cucumber. Traditionally borage flowers were used to flavor wine drinks. Candied, the flowers were popular sweets in the last century. Lift the flowers from the hairy sepals before using them. The flowers are beautiful frozen in ice cubes then floated in a refreshing summer drink.

As you can see from the recipes, borage pairs well with nasturtiums. Not only are their colors complementary—sky blue and bright orange—their flavors harmonize well.

CULTURE

Borage grows best in full sun and will tolerate a range of soils, but it prefers a light, poor, dry soil.

Direct seed borage into the garden after all danger of frost is past. The roots are very delicate, making borage difficult to transplant. Once planted the seed germinates quickly. Allow at least twelve inches between plants, more in warmer climates. Unless you harvest all the flowers, you don't have to worry about planting borage in subsequent years as it self-seeds freely.

Consider planting borage at the top of a hill or mound or on sloping ground where you can view it from below. An upward view of the plant best shows off the beauty of the drooping flowers.

WARNING

Borage can have a diuretic effect, so it should not be eaten in great quantity. It can also stimulate lactation in pregnant and nursing women.

BLUEBERRY, STRAWBERRY AND CUCUMBER COMPOTE

1/3 cup brown sugar

1 cup sour cream

1 pint blueberries, washed and stemmed

1 pint strawberries, washed, stemmed and cut in half

2 medium cucumbers, peeled, seeded and cut into 1/2-inch pieces

borage flowers

Combine brown sugar and sour cream. Add berries and cucumber. Refrigerate until time to serve. Garnish generously with borage flowers.

Serves 6 to 8.

BURGUNDY BORAGE PUNCH

from Pat Lanza, The Potager, Wurtsboro, New York

1 quart burgundy, chilled

1 quart orange-flavored seltzer, chilled

borage flowers

Mix burgundy and seltzer in a punch bowl. Float borage flowers on the punch. For a festive look, freeze borage flowers in ice cubes and float these in the punch.

Serves 12 to 16 (small punch glasses).

CALENDULA

CALENDULA
(Pot marigold)
Calendula officinalis
Composite family
Asteraceae
Slightly bitter flavor
Annual
Rich loam
Cool weather

The word calendula is derived from the Latin *calens* meaning the first day of each month. Christians called it "marygold" and "marybud" because it bloomed at all the festivals celebrating the Virgin Mary.

It is important to know a plant by its botanic name. This is even more important than the common name, as the common name can be variable in different regions, countries, and certainly in different languages. The botanic name is the same throughout the world. Calendula is an excellent case in point. It often is referred to as pot marigold. In some older books the name was shortened to marigold, leaving the reader in confusion as to whether the plant referred to was *Calendula officinalis*, or one of the many *Tagetes* species (marigolds).

The culinary use of calendula dates back to ancient Rome. The use of saffron (the powdered stigmas of the exotic saffron flower) was a sign of wealth and power. The common people couldn't afford to buy saffron, and they discovered that powdered calendula petals were an excellent substitute.

Calendula is native to Asia and southern Europe and was brought to America by the early settlers. It was introduced to Britain by the Romans.

Calendula is a flowering annual that grows to a height of twelve to eighteen inches. The stem is slightly fuzzy, and the leaves are soft, growing to six inches long. Flowers may be yellow or orange. The flowers are about one and one-half inches in diameter, consisting of concentric rows of ray florets surrounding the smaller ones making up the center disc. 'Kablouna,' a recent hybrid, has long-lasting, vibrant orange flowers. For all their beauty, calendula flowers have no fragrance.

The petals can be dried and kept in a tightly sealed container in a cool, dry place for use out of season. To dry flowers, place them on a piece of canvas or cheesecloth stretched over a screen in a warm, dry, shady place. Do not let the flowers touch one another. Once the flowers are completely dried, pick the petals off by hand and put them in a container and seal it tightly. Before adding dried petals to a recipe, pulverize them.

The flavor of calendula is slightly bitter. The petals are more often used for the color they impart than for their flavor. Calendula has been called "poor man's saffron," as the petals can be used in place of saffron in recipes. Petals must be well bruised to give off any color. The easiest way to do this is to chop the fresh petals finely.

CULTURE

Calendulas grow in a wide range of soils, but prefer a rich loam. Direct seed calendulas in the garden once the last chance of frost has past. A second planting can be made at the beginning of July to ensure a fall harvest. Thin plants to twelve inches apart.

Calendulas do not like very hot weather. They will put on a big show of color in late spring and early summer. If the summer is not too hot, they may bloom intermittently. If you deadhead the plant religiously in spring and summer, it may give another burst of color as the weather turns cooler.

ORANGE CAKE

Cake batter:

5 eggs

1/2 cup butter, softened to room temperature

1-1/2 cups granulated sugar

rind of 2 lemons, grated

rind of 1 orange, grated

1 cup sour cream

1/2 cup plain yogurt

3 cups all-purpose flour

2 teaspoons baking soda

1/2 cup calendula petals, chopped

Preheat oven to 350°F. Separate eggs. Beat whites until they form stiff peaks. Set aside.

Cream butter and sugar together. Blend in egg yolks, lemon rind, orange rind, sour cream and yogurt. Beat until smooth.

Sift dry ingredients together. Slowly add dry ingredients to wet, mixing well. Gently fold in beaten egg whites and calendula petals.

Butter and flour a Bundt cake or angel food cake pan. Pour in cake batter and bake for 60 minutes. Remove from oven and let cool in pan 10 minutes, then remove to a cooling rack and allow to cool completely.

Syrup topping:

1/2 cup orange juice

1/4 cup lemon juice

1/4 cup Grand Marnier

1/4 cup granulated sugar

Combine all ingredients in a saucepan over a low heat. Bring to a boil, then simmer for 3 minutes. Pour hot syrup over cooled cake and garnish with calendula petals.

Serves 8 to 12.

CHAMOMILE

CHAMOMILE
(English chamomile)
Chamaemelum nobile
Composite family
Asteraceae
Sweet apple flavor
Perennial (Zones 4–8)
Moist, well-drained soil
Full sun to partial shade

Chamomile has been cultivated for over two thousand years as an ornamental groundcover. In the Victorian language of flowers, it denotes energy in adversity, perhaps from its ability to rise again after being stepped on in the garden.

Chamomile is a creeping perennial herb, the plant itself growing only about one inch high. The leaves are fernlike and can form a mat around the rooting spot of the creeping plant stem. When in bloom, the flowering stems reach up to twelve inches in height. The flowers are small and daisylike with white petals surrounding a conical yellow disc. With successive pickings, the flowers will grace the garden from midsummer until they are killed by the frost of autumn.

The dried flowers are used in their entirety to make tea. Long used by herbalists as a calmative for the stomach and nerves, chamomile does indeed have mild sedative properties.

CULTURE
Chamomile grows best in moist, well-drained soil in full sun or partial shade, but it will survive in poor soil as long as it is well drained. Chamomile is easily grown from seed planted in the spring. Once established, chamomile will self-seed. In an established planting, you can divide the runners in early spring.

Harvest the flowers just when the petals begin to droop slightly. Lay the flowers on a sheet or a screen (with a cloth below to catch whatever falls through) in the sun so they can dry quickly. As they are drying, remove the leaves and stems. Once completely dried, store the flowers in a tightly covered container in a cool dry place.

WARNING
Ragweed sufferers may also be allergic to chamomile. Chamomile contains thuaone and should be drunk in moderation—no more than one cup of tea a day.

CHAMOMILE TEA

1 teaspoon dried chamomile flowers
1 cup boiling water

Let flowers steep in water for 3 to 5 minutes.

Serves 1.

DANDELION

The name is derived from the French *dent de lion*, which translates to lion's tooth, denoting the toothed edges of the leaves. The diuretic effect is evidenced from one of the common names, pissabed. In the language of flowers, dandelion denotes love's oracle.

Often looked upon disparagingly as the scourge of the perfect, well-manicured American lawn, dandelions were cultivated in European kitchen gardens for hundreds of years. The dandelion was purposely brought from Europe to the New World by the settlers.

Native Americans and the American pioneers made great use of all parts of the plant. Even today, the dandelion's versatility is widely enjoyed. Flowers are brewed into tea, wine and beer. The young leaves are delicious in salads or cooked as a green. The roots are often roasted and ground into a coffee substitute. Medicinally, the tea is used as a mild calmative.

Dandelions appear in the spring. The leaves are in a basal rosette, growing up to 12 inches long. The flowers are bright, buttercup yellow, borne singly on hollow stems that range in height from one to eighteen inches. Flower heads also vary in size from one-half to two and one-half inches in diameter, with several concentric rows of short yellow bracts.

Dandelion blossoms have a sweet, honeylike flavor when picked young. As the flowers mature, the flavor becomes bitter. The green sepals can also be somewhat bitter and should be removed for any recipe in which emphasis is placed on the sweet nature of the plant and for

DANDELION
(Pissabed, pries' crown, telltime)
Taraxacum officinale
Composite family
Asteraceae
(Cichorium Tribe)
Sweet flavor
Perennial (Zones 5–9)
Rich, well-drained soil
Cool, sun

any brewed beverage. The flowers open in the morning and close at night, so pick dandelions immediately before using them as the flowers also close quickly after picking.

CULTURE

The dandelion is a cosmopolitan herb. It was introduced from Europe to North America so long ago it is considered by some to be a native plant. Dandelions can be found growing wild throughout most of North America in grassy waste areas and on open ground.

For best leaf and flower production, sow seeds in the spring in rich, well-drained soil. Plant twelve inches apart in hills or drills. Seed can be collected from choice plants growing in the wild, although the purity is not guaranteed. For serious cultivation purposes, it is best to rely on purchased seed. I have noticed more and more dandelions appearing on lawns over the past several springs. This is in direct correlation with a decreased use of herbicides. With their bright flowers, they lend a cheery note to the otherwise stern appearance of formal lawns.

Dandelions are temperature and weather sensitive. Flowers appear in abundance during the cool clear days of mid-spring, and disappear when the weather gets hot. In the cool of autumn, a second flush of bloom appears.

Dandelions have long taproots, making them difficult to control. Digging up a portion of the plant while leaving any part of the root does not succeed in killing it. Pick the flowers before they go to seed to prevent additional seeding by the wind. Or, if you wish to spread dandelions, gently blow on the seed head and watch the featherlike seeds take flight.

WARNING

Contact dermatitis has been reported from handling dandelions. This is most likely from the latex in the leaves and stems.

Do not eat dandelions from lawns that have been chemically treated with herbicides, preemergents or weed-and-feed type fertilizers.

DANDELION WINE

4 quarts dandelion flowers (remove stem and sepals)
4 quarts granulated sugar
4 quarts boiling water
juice from 2 lemons
juice from 1 orange
1 yeast cake

Add dandelion flowers to a large stone crock or jar. Cover with sugar. Add boiling water. When water has cooled to lukewarm, add the lemon juice and orange juice. Break up the yeast cake and add to the liquid. Stir well. Cover loosely and let stand for 24 hours. Strain through cheesecloth and discard solids. Return liquid to the crock, loosely cover and let stand for 3 days.

Strain through several layers of cheesecloth. Return liquid to crock and allow to ferment. Bottle when all fermentation action stops. Keep at least 3 to 4 months before drinking.

Makes 1-1/2 gallons of wine.

IANTHUS

Dianthus literally means flower of the gods. In the Victorian language of flowers clove pink means make haste. Pinks were especially popular in kitchens of England and France in the sixteenth and seventeenth centuries. They were used in cordials, syrups, vinegars, butters and other culinary creations.

Wild clove pinks are native to the western Mediterranean. They are the horticultural parents of modern carnations.

Clove pinks are perennials hardy to zone 8. In most regions of the country they are grown as annuals. They range from one and one-half to three feet tall. Their foliage is an attractive gray blue. Pinks flourish in the cool weather of spring and fall and give out in the heat of summer.

Dianthus deltoides (maiden pink) has very small, narrow green leaves. It is low growing, forming a lovely mat in the garden. It is hardy to zone 4. The forked stalks (four to twelve inches tall) bear red or pink (occasionally white with crimson eye) three-fourths-inch flowers.

Depending on the climate, the semi-double, rose-purple or white flowers bloom in spring or fall. Dianthus flowers have a sweet clove flavor that is quite versatile in the kitchen.

CULTURE

Clove pinks grow best in full sun. They will grow in ordinary garden soil as long as it is very well drained.

Dianthus are readily available in nurseries and garden centers. Set out the plants in the spring after any danger of frost is past. Allow eight to twelve inches between plants.

DIANTHUS
(Clove pink, pinks,
carnation, gillyflower)
Dianthus caryophyllus
Pink family
Caryophyllaceae
Sweet clove flavor
Tender perennial (Zones
8–10)
Ordinary garden soil, well
drained
Full sun

Dianthus can be grown from seed sown outdoors in late spring or early summer. Seed can be sown indoors four weeks before the last frost date in spring. Seeds take two to three weeks to germinate.

Do not mulch dianthus as they need good air circulation around their roots.

Established plants can be divided in spring and replanted. You can wait and divide and replant in summer after they finish blooming.

Encourage repeat bloom by cutting off all faded flowers.

WARNING

Remove the narrow base of the petal (usually white in color) before eating as it is often bitter.

EDIBLE FLOWERS

DIANTHUS TEA

1 tablespoon dianthus petals, chopped

1 cup boiling water

Steep petals in a cup of water for 3 to 5 minutes. Strain.

Serves 1.

PINK MARMALADE

1 cup granulated sugar

1 cup water

2 cups dianthus petals, coarsely chopped

Put sugar and water into a heavy, nonaluminum saucepan. Bring to a boil and simmer until it thickens to a syrup consistency. Add chopped petals and gently simmer, stirring frequently, until pulpy. Pour into sterilized jars and allow to cool to room temperature. Refrigerate for up to 3 weeks.

DIANTHUS SORBET

2 cups water

1/4 cup granulated sugar

1/2 cup dianthus petals, coarsely chopped

Pour water into a nonaluminum saucepan. Add granulated sugar and petals, stirring well to dissolve sugar. Bring liquid to a boil, turn down heat and allow to simmer for 5 minutes. Remove from heat and let cool to room temperature. Pour into an ice cream maker and process according to manufacturer's directions. Freeze until ready to serve.

Serves 4 to 6.

*E*LDERBERRY

The word elder is derived from the Anglo-Saxon *aeld*, meaning fire. The hollow branches of the plant were blown through to increase the flames of fires. Pliny used the name *sambucus* to describe this plant two thousand years ago. It is derived from the Greek *sambuca* referring to the Roman woodwind instrument. It is interesting to note that western American Indians called it *(Sambucus caerulea)* "the tree of music," as they bored a hole through the pith to make a flute. They also used the long shoots for arrow shafts.

Mythically, the elder is considered to be the witch's tree. Supposedly it is a favored form for a witch to assume. You could tell if your plant was a witch, as it would bleed if it were cut. Many superstitions surrounded the plant; people were hesitant to cut one down or burn it. Some people planted elderberries around their houses to protect against witches and in graveyards to guide happiness to the deceased.

Evidence of elderberry cultivation has been found in Stone Age sites in Switzerland and Italy. Elderberry *(Sambucus canadensis)* can be found growing wild in rich soils from Nova Scotia to Georgia and Texas to Manitoba. *Sambucus caerulea* grows in open areas from California to western Canada.

Elderberry is a large deciduous shrub, which can easily grow to ten feet in height. The stems have a thick white pith. The leaves are compound, growing opposite on the branches. Each leaflet is oval and toothed, with five or seven comprising a leaf.

ELDERBERRY
Sambucus canadensis
and S. caerulea
Honeysuckle family
Caprifoliaceae
Sweet flavor
Shrub (Zones 3–8)
Rich, well-drained soil
Full sun

The small white or off-white flowers, often called elderblow, appear in flat umbrellalike clusters in June and July. By late summer the berries ripen, turning purplish black.

The flowers are delightfully sweet scented and sweet tasting. When harvesting elderberry flowers, do not wash them as that removes much of the fragrance and flavor. Instead, check them carefully for insects.

CULTURE
Elderberry prefers moist, sheltered areas in which to grow. Plant in full sun in rich, moist, but well-drained soil.

Plants can be purchased at nurseries or garden centers. Water well after planting. Once established, an elderberry needs little care.

EDIBLE FLOWERS

WARNING

The leaves, bark, branches and roots of elderberries contain poisonous alkaloids. Only the flowers, not even the stems of the recommended elderberries, should be eaten. The berries should only be eaten after they have been cooked or processed as with wine or jam, never eaten raw. Even the flowers should not be consumed directly from the plant.

The tea can act as a mild laxative or promote sweating in some individuals; drink it in moderation.

ELDERBLOW TEA

elder blossoms
water to cover
lemon wedges
honey

In a nonmetallic container, cover the elder blossoms with cold water. Allow them to soak for 24 hours. Strain and discard the flowers. Dilute with water to taste. Serve with a squeeze of lemon and sweeten with honey to taste.

ELDERBLOW MINT TEA

1 cup elderblow
3 sprigs mint
4 cups water

Add elderblow and mint to boiling water. Steep for 10 minutes. Strain. Delicious served hot or cold. This drink is supposedly good to calm a queasy stomach.

ELDERBLOW MUFFINS

1 cup unbleached flour, sifted
2 teaspoons baking powder
1/2 teaspoon salt
1/4 cup granulated sugar
1 1/2 cups elderblow
2 tablespoons sweet (unsalted) butter, melted
1 egg, beaten
1/2 cup buttermilk
1/2 cup orange juice

Preheat oven to 400°F. Sift together dry ingredients into a bowl. Toss in flowers. In a separate bowl, mix butter, egg, buttermilk and orange juice. Add wet mixture to dry, stirring only until dry ingredients are moistened.

Grease muffin tins. Fill each cup 2/3 with batter. Bake 20 to 25 minutes until muffins are lightly brown.

Makes 24 muffins.

ENGLISH DAISY

Despite its name, the English daisy is native to Eurasia. It has been widely cultivated in northern Europe and England.

This plant is to the English what the dandelion is to Americans, a rather invasive lawn weed. Ironically, in England dandelions are cultivated plants widely available in nurseries, while in America, English daisies are cultivated. In California and the Pacific Northwest, however, the weather is mild enough for these perennial beauties to seed themselves into lawns occasionally, yet they are still not looked upon as a scourge the way dandelions are.

English daisies are perennials that grow to six inches tall. The leaves are at the base of the plant, forming a tuft. The flower heads grow singly on thin stalks. Flower heads average between one and two inches across with white, pink or red ray flowers surrounding the center of yellow disk flowers. English daisies bloom in the spring and early summer. Single, semi-double and double flowers are available.

The ray flowers have a mildly bitter taste and are more commonly used for their looks than their flavor.

CULTURE

English daisies prefer to grow in full sun and moist soil. They thrive in cool weather.

ENGLISH DAISY
Bellis perennis
Composite family
Asteraceae
Bitter flavor
Perennial (Zones 4–9)
Moist soil
Full sun

Although they are technically perennial, in cold areas they are often treated as tender annuals or biennials. In warm areas, they are treated as hardy biennials.

In warm areas with mild winters, sow seed directly in the garden in late summer. This will give a lovely show of color for winter and spring. In areas with cold winters, start the seeds indoors in midwinter. Grow them in temperatures between fifty-five and sixty-five degrees Fahrenheit. Transplant into the garden as soon as the soil can be worked. Place a light mulch of soil over the plants until all danger of frost is past. In this manner, you will have a show of color for late spring.

Pick off spent flowers. If the summer is cool, a second flush of bloom can occur in late summer or early autumn.

SUNSHINE CAKE

from Applewood Seed Company, Golden, Colorado

2-1/4 cups all-purpose flour, sifted
2-1/2 teaspoons baking powder
1 teaspoon salt
2/3 cup butter, softened
1-1/2 cups granulated sugar
3 eggs
1 cup milk
1-1/2 teaspoons vanilla
2 9-inch round cake pans, greased and floured

Frosting:
1/2 cup butter, softened
8 ounces cream cheese, softened
4 cups confectioners' sugar, sifted
1 teaspoon vanilla
1 teaspoon jasmine essence (optional—available in Middle-Eastern or Oriental markets. If not available, substitute orange flower water or rose water.)
English daisy petals

Preheat oven to 350°F. In a bowl, sift together flour, baking powder and salt. Set aside. In a separate bowl, cream butter and sugar until the mixture is light and fluffy. Add eggs, beating thoroughly. Alternately add flour mixture and milk, beating well after each addition. Stir in vanilla. Pour into buttered and floured pans. Bake 20 to 30 minutes or until a toothpick inserted in the center of each cake comes out clean. Place pans on a cooling rack for 10 minutes. Remove cakes from pans, cool completely on rack.

In a bowl, cream together butter and cream cheese. Gradually add sugar, beating continually. Add vanilla and jasmine essence. Beat until smooth. Frost cake. Garnish cake with English daisy petals.

fENNEL

One of the superstitions surrounding fennel is that anyone who eats it will have clearer vision. Like dill, fennel was also a symbol of victory to the ancient Greeks and Romans. For centuries fennel was used ritualistically, and later medicinally. It was not until the fourteenth century that fennel seed began to be appreciated as a culinary herb. The rich used it to flavor fish and vegetables, while the poor used it as an appetite suppressant on fast days.

Originally native to the Mediterranean area, fennel is now cultivated worldwide. Fennel was first brought to North America by Spanish priests, evidenced by it growing wild around old missions. Today fennel has also naturalized along roadsides from Connecticut to Florida, and from Nebraska to Michigan. In the Southwest, especially in California, it has become a common weed.

Fennel is a perennial herb that is often grown as an annual. Fennel and dill are sometimes confused, but a closer look reveals the differences. Both are graceful looking plants to have in the garden. Fennel's stems are blue green, glossy and somewhat flattened at the base. The foliage is bright green and feathery. The clusters of tiny yellow flowers in flat-topped umbels do not appear until the summer of the second year. By fall the flowers have matured, producing one-quarter-inch gray green seeds (actually fruits) that are much used in Indian and other cookery.

The plant itself gives off a strong anise scent. It is beautiful in flower arrangements and keeps its scent for days.

FENNEL
Foeniculum vulgare
Carrot family
Apiaceae
Anise flavor
Perennial (Zones 5–9)
Average garden soil
Partial shade to full sun

CULTURE

Fennel grows happily in average garden soil. Fennel can grow four to six feet tall. Plant it along the north side of the garden to keep it from casting shade on other plants.

In mild areas of the country, sow seed of fennel in early spring. In colder areas, seed fennel into the garden in July. Of course, like many of the other herbs, small plants are available at nurseries and garden centers. They can be planted anytime in spring after danger of frost is past. Allow at least eight inches between plants.

Bronze fennel is somewhat lower growing than wild fennel and more compact in its habit. A row of it is very handsome in the vegetable garden. I have seen a grouping of three or more bronze fennel in a perennial border—the effect is striking, indeed. In western gardens, bronze fennel thrives as a hardy perennial.

The flavor of fennel flowers is mildly anise.

WARNING

Fennel or the seed oil may cause contact dermatitis in sensitive individuals.

APPLE PIE

1/2 cup granulated sugar

1/3 cup brown sugar

2 tablespoons all-purpose flour

2 tablespoons fennel florets, finely chopped

6 tart apples, peeled and sliced thinly

pastry for a 9-inch pie crust in pie pan

2 tablespoons butter

Preheat oven to 375°F. In a bowl, combine sugar, brown sugar, flour and fennel florets. Toss in the apples. Add mixture to pie pan. Cut butter into small pieces and dot over apples. Bake for about 35 to 45 minutes, or until apples are cooked.

The fennel flowers give this traditional dish a new twist.

Serves 6 to 8.

HIBISCUS

Hibiscus rosa-sinensis is among the most widely culti-vated of the more than three hundred different species of hibiscus. Native to tropical Asia, hibiscus is now found growing in tropical and subtropical areas worldwide.

Chinese hibiscus is an evergreen, growing as a small tree or large shrub. In the wild it can grow to thirty feet high; in cultivation it grows to a more controllable four to fifteen feet. The deep green, glossy, oval leaves are somewhat pointed and slightly toothed on the edges. Leaves range from one to four inches long.

The flowers are large and exotic looking. When fully open the flared, five-petaled flower can be four to six inches across with brilliantly hued petals of orange, red or purplish red. The reproductive parts of the flowers stick out on a long filament, adding to their exotic beauty. Usually each flower only lasts for a day or two, but new buds are constantly produced, making the hibiscus almost everblooming.

Hibiscus' main culinary contribution is the luscious red color and mild citrus/cranberry flavor that it imparts to teas.

CULTURE

Hibiscus rosa-sinensis is hardy in zones 9 and 10. Else-where it must be grown in a container. It can be taken outdoors for the summer. As it is not frost hardy, it must be

HIBISCUS (China rose, Chinese hibiscus, rose-of-China, Chinese rose, Hawaiian hibiscus)
Hibiscus rosa-sinensis
Mallow family
Malvaceae
Mild citrus flavor
Small tree (Zones 9–10)
Well-drained soil
Full sun

brought back inside before the cold weather sets in. It can be kept indoors year-round in a greenhouse.

Hibiscus grows best in full sun and well-drained soil. Protect it from the wind by growing it in a sheltered location. To achieve a full, lushly formed plant, prune the hibiscus stems back by one-third of their length each spring.

There is a good choice of hibiscus cultivars available commercially, subsequently hibiscus is not often propagated by amateur growers. Softwood cuttings can be taken in the summer. Because most hibiscus are hybrids, growing them from seed does not often result in plants true to the parent.

HIBISCUS TEA

1 tablespoon hibiscus petals, fresh, or 1 teaspoon dried
1 cup boiling water
honey (optional)

Steep petals in water in a cup for 5 minutes. For additional sweetness add honey, if desired.

Serves 1.

HONEYSUCKLE

HONEYSUCKLE
(Wild honeysuckle,
Japanese honeysuckle)
Lonicera japonica
Honeysuckle family
Caprifoliaceae
Floral flavor
Perennial vine (Zones 3–8)
Any soil
Full sun

In the Victorian language of flowers, honeysuckle denotes affection. If, as an adult, you try to recreate some wonderful childhood memory, it often falls short of your expectation. Not only that, but the less than wonderful adult experience manages to tarnish the childhood memory. I had not tasted honeysuckle in over thirty years, so it was with more than slight trepidation that I went to try this childhood favorite. As I bit into the end of the flower, I could sense the presence of the nectar. The aroma and sweet flavor were just as I had remembered. That is the good news about honeysuckle.

Honeysuckle was imported into America from Japan around the turn of the century. It was highly touted as a decorative climber. Indeed it is both decorative and climbing, however, now it is considered to be a pernicious weed. It is described as an evergreen, twining vine that climbs or covers the ground, self-rooting as it goes. The vine can easily grow to thirty feet in length. The stems are slightly hairy. The two- to three-inch leaves, which grow opposite on the stems, have a somewhat narrow heart shape. The leaves are deep green, often downy below, but less commonly downy above.

The flowers appear in May and continue to bloom sporadically through late summer. When the first flush of bloom is on the vine, the scent wafts through the air, especially at night. That is the time to discover where the honeysuckle is growing; its sweet perfume will lead you to the plant. The flowers are trumpet-shaped, growing in pairs. The flowers start off white, occasionally tinged purple, and turn buff yellow as they mature.

At the base of the flower is the cache of nectar, which is actually what gives the sweet flavor. Carefully break a tiny piece at the base of the flower, without breaking the filament. Slowly pull the piece away from the flower, bringing the filament toward you. Just as it reaches the base of the flower you see a drop of golden nectar. Touch it to your tongue. What a sensual delight! That is the same flavor you get when you eat the entire flower: a floral, nectarous delectation.

In Japan, the flowers are used to make a beverage tea, available commercially in Asian markets.

CULTURE

There is more information in the literature on how to control and eradicate Japanese honeysuckle than there is on how to grow it. Although it is beautiful growing up a trellis or bower, the risk is too great that this plant will get out of bounds. Once it does, it can spread rapidly in open sunny areas or under (and around and up) trees as well, strangling anything in its path.

Don't grow it, but take advantage of it where you do find it and enjoy the flowers. Share them with your children and your parents. Everyone should know the joy of tasting a honeysuckle.

WARNING

Only *Lonicera japonica* is edible. Although the many other varieties of honeysuckle are recommended as ornamental in the garden, do not eat them.

HONEYSUCKLE STRAWBERRY SORBET

1/2 cup honeysuckle flowers
3 cups strawberries, cleaned, hulled and cut in half

Cut pistils and stamens out of honeysuckle flower, being careful not to remove the nectar at the base of the flower. Put flowers and strawberries into the bowl of a food processor fitted with the metal blade. Process until smooth.

Pour mixture into an ice cream maker and freeze according to manufacturer's directions. Serve garnished with several honeysuckle flowers.

An ambrosial dessert with no added sugar. The honeysuckle is in peak bloom at the same time the local strawberries are ripe, making a wonderful marriage of flavors.

Serves 6 to 8.

JASMINE

JASMINE
(Arabian jasmine)
Jasminum sambac
Olive family
Oleaceae
Vine (Zone 10)
Sweet perfumed flavor
Well-drained soil
Bright light

The roots of Arabian jasmine are probably in tropical Asia, but it has been cultivated for thousands of years and its true history has become lost.

Jasmine is a vining plant, hardy only in zone 10. In all other areas, it can be grown as a houseplant that blooms in winter. The tubular, white flowers are borne in clusters in the winter. The flowers are intensely fragrant and are traditionally used for scenting tea.

CULTURE

Grow jasmine in bright light, with several hours of full sun a day. It prefers temperatures of sixty degrees Fahrenheit at night and eighty degrees Fahrenheit during the day. Keep the plant lightly moist in spring and summer; feed every two weeks. In fall and winter, allow the soil to dry out a bit between waterings; do not fertilize. In spring, prune the stems back and repot the plant. Jasmine can be propagated from tip cuttings in summer or fall.

WARNING

Do not confuse jasmine with the poisonous Carolina jasmine (*Gelsemium sempervierens*) or Jessamine (*Cestrum* spp.).

JASMINE TEA

tea leaves (choose a strongly flavored tea)
jasmine flowers

For a mildly fragrant tea, use 6 to 8 parts tea to 1 part jasmine flowers. Mix tea leaves with jasmine flowers in a bowl. Place in a jar and cover with cheesecloth and allow to stand for a week or more in a cool, dry area or until jasmine flowers have dried out and infused the tea with their perfume.

JOHNNY-JUMP-UP

In the Victorian language of flowers, the three colors of the Johnny-jump-up—purple, white and yellow—denote memories, loving thoughts and souvenirs. Sent to ease the hearts of separated lovers, it acquired the name heartsease. It also was a regular ingredient in love potions.

Johnny-jump-ups were introduced to America from their native Europe. They have escaped from gardens and now grow in fields, wastelands and along forest edges throughout much of North America.

Although Johnny-jump-ups are annuals, they seem to be perennial. They produce numerous seeds that germinate quickly, ensuring that this feisty plant will continue in the garden year after year. Notice that this year's plants may be in different parts of the garden from last year—Johnny has jumped up again.

They grow from four to twelve inches high with toothed leaves, rounded near the bottom of the plant, oblong higher on the plant. The five-petaled flowers resemble cute little (one-half to one inch) faces, smiling at you from the garden.

The petals by themselves have almost no flavor. If the flower is eaten in its entirety (including green sepals), there is a distinct wintergreen flavor to the flower. One grower remarked that it tasted just like Pepto-Bismol. The flowers are beautiful candied or floated on punch. The mild flavor makes them versatile and at home in a fruit salad or on a veal chop.

JOHNNY-JUMP-UP
(Heartsease, field pansy)
Viola tricolor
Violet family
Violaceae
Mint flavor
Annual/self-seeds
Ordinary soil
Full sun to shade

CULTURE

In warm areas of the country, sow seed in fall for bloom throughout the winter. In areas that get frost, seed sown in fall will germinate early in spring. In the cold areas, seed can also be directly sown in the garden early in spring. Seed can be started in winter indoors and the plants transplanted outdoors in spring. Once established in the garden, Johnny-jump-ups will self-seed and delight you with their cheery countenances for years.

Johnny-jump-ups prefer cool weather and bloom profusely in the spring. Keep them deadheaded, and if the summer is not too hot they may revive in the fall.

WARNING

Johnny-jump-ups contain saponins and may be toxic in large amounts.

SPRING FRUIT SALAD

2 oranges, peeled, sectioned and cut into bite-sized pieces

1 medium bunch of green seedless grapes

1 pint strawberries, stems removed, cut in half

1 tart apple, cut into bite-sized pieces

2 kiwis, peeled and sliced thinly

20 Johnny-jump-up flowers

Mix fruits in a nonmetallic bowl several hours before serving, allowing the flavors to meld. Serve garnished with the Johnny-jump-up flowers.

Serves 4.

LAVENDER

The word lavender comes from the Latin *lavare*, meaning to wash. The ancient Greeks and Romans used lavender for its fresh clean scent in washing water, in soaps and for perfuming sheets. These uses have persisted for several millennia. During the Middle Ages it was a popular strewing herb. Much legend surrounds lavender, and over the years it has been imbued with certain powers by diverse peoples. In North Africa lavender is used to protect the Kabyle women from being mistreated by their husbands, while in Tuscany it protects small children from the evil eye. Its ability to soothe and calm, merely from its scent, is supposed to work on animals and humans alike. To the Victorians in their language of flowers, lavender meant distrust.

Lavender is originally native to the Mediterranean mountains and coast. Lavender is a shrubby plant, multibranched with woody branches and narrow leaves. The fragrant flowers appear on the ends of long spikes. The conquering Romans first brought lavender to England, where it continues to grow happily. Bees are attracted to lavender; lavender honey is a gourmand's delight. The most popular use of lavender is for fragrance. It is used in perfume, soap and toiletries. Sachets line linen closets and lingerie drawers throughout the world.

Lavandula angustifolia, English or true lavender, is the best for eating. This same plant has been known as *Lavandula officinalis* and *Lavandula vera*. It is a hardier perennial than the French lavender. English lavender has blunt,

LAVENDER
Lavandula *spp.*
Mint family
Lamiaceae
Perfumed flavor
Shrub (Zones 6–10)
Light, dry, well-drained soil
Full sun

narrow, grayish green leaves. In warm climates it can grow to three feet or more. The small lavender flowers are grouped in whorls of six to ten.

French lavender (*Lavandula stoechas*) has long, narrow, grayish green leaves. Its flowers are a rich dark purple. It is smaller, growing to about twelve inches tall, and thrives in warm climates.

Lavender flowers have a sweet, perfumed flavor with a lemon overtone. Lavender can be very intense, so use it sparingly. Too much can give a soapy flavor.

CULTURE
Lavender prefers a sunny location and light, dry, well-drained soil. It is an ideal plant for a large rock garden.

The easiest way to grow lavender is to purchase a young plant from a nursery in the spring. Set it out in the garden after any danger of frost is past. Allow at least twelve to eighteen inches between plants. In the first year, cut off any flowering stems as they appear. This encourages the plant to grow more foliage and become bushier. Such treatment seems severe, but in the long run you will have a healthier, more vigorous plant.

If you are patient, however, you can grow it from seed. In the Northeast, where I live, I have not had great luck with lavender from seed, with a successful germination rate of about twenty-five to forty percent. Not all the plants that germinated survived, but I am particularly proud of those that did. Plant seed in late fall. It is slow to germinate, so don't give up. In northern areas, the seeds may not germinate until the following spring. By summer, the seedlings can be transplanted.

Lavender is marginally hardy in cold areas. Mulch the plants well in late autumn to protect them through the winter. Space permitting, plants can be moved indoors for the winter and grown on a sunny windowsill or under lights. Lavender often begins to look ratty after about four years. The simplest solution is to replace the plant.

Lavender flowers can be used fresh or dried. To dry, pick the flower stems when the buds begin to open or when in full bloom. Place them on a clean cloth stretched over a screen. Dry the tops in the shade. Stems can also be hung upside down to dry, wrapped in a layer of cheesecloth, in a shady place. Once dried, it is easy to pluck the flowers from the stems. Store flowers in a tightly covered container in a dry place, or freeze for future use.

WARNING

Lavender oil may be poisonous. No more than two undiluted drops should be taken internally.

LAVENDER ICE CREAM

1-1/2 cups milk

1-1/2 cups cream

1-inch section of vanilla bean, sliced lengthwise

6 egg yolks

1/3 cup granulated sugar

2 tablespoons lavender flowers, finely chopped

In a saucepan, heat milk and cream to a scald. Add vanilla bean. Remove pan from heat and allow to cool slightly. In the top of a double boiler, whisk egg yolks and sugar. Slowly pour in the milk, whisking constantly. Continue to cook until the mixture begins to thicken and coats a wooden spoon. Add lavender flowers. Remove from heat and allow to cool to room temperature for at least one hour. Chill in the refrigerator for one hour. Strain liquid and pour into an ice cream maker and freeze according to manufacturer's instructions.

Serves 4 to 6.

LAVENDER COOKIES

———

from José Gutierrez, executive chef, Chez Philippe, Peabody Hotel, Memphis, Tennessee

2/3 cup granulated sugar

3/4 cup all-purpose flour

4 egg whites

1/2 cup butter, melted

1/2 teaspoon vanilla

3 tablespoons lavender florets, chopped

Preheat oven to 450°F. In a mixing bowl, blend sugar and flour. Whisk in egg whites, one at a time. Whisk butter into mixture. Add vanilla. Refrigerate for 10 minutes.

Lightly oil a cookie sheet. For simple cookies, pour 1 to 2 teaspoons of batter onto the cookie sheet, allowing 1 inch between each cookie. For curlicues, pipe the batter, using a pastry bag, onto the cookie sheet, making 9-inch-long strips 1/4-inch wide, allowing 1 inch between each strip. Bake in preheated oven 1 minute. Remove from oven and sprinkle florets on each cookie, once the batter has spread out. Return to oven and bake for several minutes until very lightly browned. Remove one cookie at a time, wrapping it around a 1-inch diameter cylinder (large pencil). Cookies cool quickly and become brittle.

ORANGE AND LAVENDER SORBET

———

from José Gutierrez, executive chef, Chez Philippe, Peabody Hotel, Memphis, Tennessee

1 quart freshly squeezed orange juice, divided

9 ounces granulated sugar

1 tablespoon lavender flowers, finely chopped

In a nonaluminum saucepan heat 2 cups of orange juice with the sugar. Stir to mix. Add lavender flowers and bring to a boil. Lower heat and simmer for 15 minutes. Strain. Pour the liquid into the remaining 2 cups of orange juice and mix. Pour the mixture into an ice cream maker and process according to manufacturer's instructions. When frozen, scoop into glasses and serve garnished with additional chopped lavender. Pour a splash of Cointreau on top for an interesting variation.

Serves 6 to 8.

LEMON

LEMON
Citrus limon
Rue family
Rutaceae
Citrus flavor
Tree (Zones 9 and 10)
Light, fertile loam
Full sun

The name is derived from the Arabic and Persian word *limun* used for all citrus fruits. In the Victorian language of flowers, lemon means fidelity.

Lemons were believed to have been introduced to the western world from India in the tenth century. Recently lemons have been identified in the ruins of Pompeii, leading to the assumption that lemons had been cultivated by the Romans.

Lemons are small trees, ranging from ten to twenty feet in height, hardy to zones 9 and 10. In cooler climates, dwarf varieties can be grown in containers in a greenhouse in the winter and brought outside in the summer. Their growth habit is open, with lightly thorned branches. The semi-glossy green leaves are elliptical with crenated edges. They are attractive landscape trees in warm areas. Lemons are usually cultivated for their fruit.

Lemon flowers are very fragrant. They appear star-shaped and are less than one inch in diameter, white inside, streaked with violet outside. The flavor is citrusy and sweet.

CULTURE

Lemons need full sun. They prefer light, well-drained, fertile loam rich in organic matter.

Plant lemons in late winter or early spring. They are usually purchased from a nursery. Choose your plant well. Look for trees suitable for your climate. When planting, allow twenty to thirty-five feet around each tree. Lemons need plenty of water until well established. Water every two to five days in hot dry areas; in more humid areas, every week or two. Mulch well around the tree, taking care not to mulch right up to the trunk. Apply citrus fertilizer as directed, but do not feed after midsummer.

Lemons adapt readily to container cultivation. In cooler climates grow the plants outdoors during the warm months and indoors during the cool months. Indoors, they require bright light and cool days and nights, not over sixty-five degrees Fahrenheit for flower production. Do not allow the soil to dry out.

LEMONCELLO

from Georgene McKim, Palos Verdes, California

8 to 10 lemons

1 liter of 80- or 90-proof vodka

3 cups granulated sugar

4 cups water

20 lemon flowers

Zest lemons. Mix vodka and lemon zest. Pour into a large bottle. Cover loosely and let infuse for 1 week.

Put sugar and water in a medium saucepan. Bring to a boil. Do not stir. Boil for 15 minutes. Add lemon flowers. Allow syrup to cool to room temperature. Combine vodka with syrup and stir well. Strain into bottles and cork. Let age for 2 weeks.

Store in the freezer. Serve icy cold in thimble-sized vodka glasses, garnished with a fresh lemon flower.

LILAC

LILAC
(Common lilac)
Syringa vulgaris
Olive family
Oleaceae
Floral flavor
Shrub (Zones 4–7)
Well-drained, alkaline soil
Sun to partial shade

Lilacs are grown for the colorful fragrant display they give in spring. The individual flowers, which have four petals, are clustered together to form a spike. Flowers come in a range of purples, mauves and, of course, light purple (lilac). Hybridization has brought white flowers. Although lilacs are commonly grown and there are many cultivars, most people have no idea which variety lilac they have in their yard.

The flavor of lilacs varies from plant to plant. I have sampled many lilac flowers. Some have no flavor at all. Others have a decidedly green or herbaceous flavor. Some start out with a green flavor but have a perfumed floral aftertaste. The best lilacs are those that have the straight floral, perfumed flavor of lilac.

CULTURE

Lilacs prefer full sun but will tolerate partial shade. They grow in almost any type of soil as long as it is well drained and not alkaline. Acidic soil will prevent them from flowering.

Lilacs are widely available in the nursery trade. Plant in the spring or fall. Suckers can be dug out and replanted in early fall. Allow at least six feet between plants. Mulch lilacs with four to six inches of well-rotted manure every two years in autumn. This is the best fertilizer for these shrubs.

Lilacs benefit from regular pruning. Cut back any obviously dead wood in the winter. Remove all weak wood that does not have large flower buds or that still has the past

The word lilac is actually an Old English word which is derived from the Arabic *laylak* and Persian *nilak* meaning blue. *Syringa* is Greek for tube, referring to the shape of the individual flowers. In the language of flowers lilacs symbolize memory and humility; white lilacs symbolize innocence.

The common lilac is native to southeastern Europe. It is a beautiful flowering shrub, hardy to zone 4. It needs a period of winter cold and dormancy, and consequently cannot grow in zones 8 to 10.

Lilacs can grow, if unpruned, up to fifteen feet tall, usually in a shrubby habit. The heart-shaped leaves are an attractive green.

year's fruit on it. In the spring, the number of blooms will not be great, but each cluster will be large. The second year more flowers and bigger flowers will be produced. By the third year the clusters will be more plentiful, but will be getting smaller. Repeat the pruning process every three years.

LILAC YOGURT

1 pint frozen vanilla yogurt
1/4 cup lilac blossoms

Soften yogurt slightly and mix in flowers. Serve garnished with flowers.

This is quick and easy to prepare just before serving. If refreezing any of the yogurt, be aware that the flowers may turn brown. It will not affect the flavor, but it looks unattractive.

Serves 4.

LINDEN

LINDEN
(Basswood, lime tree)
Tilia spp.
Linden family
Tiliceae
Sweet honey flavor
Tree (Zones 3–8)
Moist loam
Full sun

The name is derived form the Greek *ptilon,* meaning wing. This refers to the large bract from which the flower arises.

American linden *(Tilia americana)* is native to most of the eastern half of North America, growing as far north as Canada, south to Florida and west to Texas. Other lindens include European linden *(Tilia x europaea),* small-leafed linden *(T. cordata)* and broad-leafed linden *(T. platyphyllos).* The different species of linden can interbreed, so it is common to find natural hybrids. For the same reason it may be difficult to identify a linden with complete accuracy.

Lindens are handsome deciduous trees that grow from forty to eighty feet or more in height. The heart-shaped leaves have sharp edges and range in size from three to nine inches. Small flowers, white to yellow in color, appear in early summer. The flower stalk comes out of a leaflike bract; the flowers are delightfully fragrant and have a honeylike flavor.

CULTURE

All lindens need full sun. *T. americana* grows in a range of soils; *T. cordata* grows best in cool, deep, moist loam; and *T. platyphyllos* prefers light soil and humid conditions. Purchase a young tree from a reputable nursery or mail-order catalog. Plant in spring or fall. Mulch well around the base of the tree but not right up to the trunk. Remember to take into account how large it will eventually grow.

WARNING

Recent studies indicate that frequent consumption of linden flower tea may cause heart damage.

LINDEN TEA

1 tablespoon linden flowers
1 cup water, boiling

Steep the flowers in water for several minutes.

Serves 1.

MINT

The exact origins of mints have been lost, with some sources suggesting that they are native to Europe, others the Mediterranean, still others the Near East, and another Hindustan. Today mints are grown around the world. There are more than twenty-five species of mint, hundreds of cultivars and unknown numbers of garden hybrids. In North America, both spearmint and peppermint have naturalized and can be found growing wild in damp places from Nova Scotia to Minnesota and south to Utah, Tennessee and Florida.

Mint is mentioned in the Bible used in lieu of money as a tithe. According to the Victorian language of flowers, mint symbolizes virtue; peppermint is warm feeling and spearmint is warmth of sentiment. Medicinally, mint has been written about since the first century A.D. Even today mint's role as a stomach palliative is evidenced by the number of after dinner drinks and candies aimed to soothe the overstuffed stomach. For centuries mint was used as a strewing herb to dispel foul odors. Today, mint is used in mouthwashes and toothpastes. The culinary uses are broader in the Middle East than in North America. Yet with our increasing interest in international cooking, dishes like tabbouleh are not totally unknown in mainstream America.

In general, mints are hardy perennials, growing from one and one-half to three feet tall. Mints are distinguished by their square stems, which often have a reddish hue.

There are many different mints, each unique in appearance as well as flavor. Try some suggested here or experiment with others you run across.

MINT
Mentha spp.
Mint family
Lamiaceae (Labiatae)
Minty flavor
Perennial (Zones 3–9)
Rich, well-drained soil, but will grow anywhere
Prefer partial shade

American apple mint (Golden apple mint)
Mentha gentilis 'Variegata'

This culinary herb has smooth, grayish green leaves variegated with yellow. It has a tendency to sprawl in the garden. In midsummer light purple flowers are borne in whorls along the stems. The flowers have a delicate, fruity, spearmint flavor.

Curly mint
Mentha spicata 'Crispa'

Curly mint has wide, crinkled, dull leaves. It spreads quickly in the garden. It grows to two feet in height, but tends to sprawl by midsummer when it blooms. The violet flowers are borne on slender spikes. It has the flavor of spearmint.

Orange mint (Bergamot mint)
Mentha citrata

Orange mint's smooth, broad, dark-green leaves are lightly edged with a touch of purple. Purple flowers appear at the tips of short spikes in midsummer. At that point, the plant often sprawls. However, this is one of the least aggressive mints, an admirable quality.

Peppermint (Lamb mint, lammint)
Mentha piperita
English black peppermint
Mentha piperita 'Vulgaris'
White peppermint
Mentha piperita 'Officinalis'

Peppermint is highly cultivated for its essential oil. Traditionally mint sauce is served with lamb, perhaps that is the origin of its other names.

Two distinct peppermints are commonly grown: black peppermint (with dark-green leaves tinged purple, purple stems and purple flowers tinged with red at the tips of long spikes) and white peppermint (with light green leaves and purple flowers at the tips of slender, long spikes). Black peppermint is taller than white. According to some experts, the oil distilled from the white peppermint is the best. Peppermint will die out if grown in the same spot in the garden for several years. Often it is a self-solving problem—the mint will run off and start growing in a new area all by itself. The flavor of the flowers is peppermint.

Spearmint
Mentha spicata

This most common mint, of julep fame, is found garnishing glasses of iced tea and lemonade throughout the summer. It grows to three feet tall; medium-green stalkless leaves are strongly toothed. The plant has a more compact habit than peppermint. The flowers, in whorls on slender spikes at the ends of stems and branches, are off-white to lavender and appear in midsummer. The flower flavor is spearmint.

CULTURE

Mints grow best in rich, moist, well-drained soil. Although they prefer partial shade, a sunny location will do. I remember mint in numerous gardens in the small beach-front community of my childhood. Very sandy soil, full sun, dry and well drained—the mints thrived. I have yet to see a growing condition that deters mint.

Mint is usually not grown from seed, but is easily propagated from roots or runners. This is very simple to do. Pull up a stem of mint and you will pull up some roots. Lay the stem in a furrow four inches deep in a shady location. I like to gently bend the top six inches so they extend above the soil. Cover the stem with soil and tamp it down. Space furrows three feet apart. In warm areas of the country, this can be done in early March; in other areas, wait until after any danger of frost is past and the ground has warmed up.

Young plants are available at nurseries, garden centers and through mail-order companies. Wait until the weather and soil warm up before planting. Allow at least twelve to eighteen inches between plants. If mint starts crowding the garden, simply pull up stems—you can always replant them elsewhere, but be aware that the stem is usually attached to an underground runner, so it will continue to flourish.

Mints are very aggressive in the garden, spreading by underground runners. Once established in a garden they can be difficult to keep within bounds. One way to control them is to grow them in containers rather than in the ground. Be careful where you place the container. After several years, a container of mint on my patio had rooted down between the flagstones and suddenly I found mint popping up all around. Another method is to grow mints as annuals, planting them in a container and then planting the container in the garden. After the patio incident, I have resorted to growing mint in a relatively large (for the size of the plant) pot without drainage holes. I then sink the pot into the garden, leaving about an inch of the rim above ground. At the end of the growing season, I take no chances and dig up the pot. Other growers suggest surrounding a planting of mint with strips of metal sunk eighteen inches into the ground.

CHAMPAGNE FRUIT TERRINE

from José Gutierrez, executive chef, Chez Philippe, Peabody Hotel, Memphis, Tennessee

6 oranges

4 grapefruit

1 cup raspberries

1 cup blueberries

2 packets plain gelatin

1 cup orange juice, strained

1 cup champagne

1/2 cup granulated sugar

10 sprigs mint flowers

Cut top and bottom off oranges and grapefruit. Cut off skin, removing any white pith, preserving the round shape. Cut the sections from the oranges and grapefruit. Place in a sieve to allow excess juice to collect in a bowl beneath. Reserve drained juice.

Layer a terrine (or a loaf pan), starting with grapefruit, then oranges, raspberries and blueberries. Repeat layers to within 1/2 inch of the top of the pan, finishing with a citrus layer.

Dissolve gelatin in 1/2 cup of orange juice over low heat. Beat sugar into remaining orange juice and champagne. Gently rub the flowers of the mint over a plate to release the florets. Some of the green sepals will release as well—that is alright. Add flowers and dissolved gelatin. Pour over fruit. Chill in refrigerator at least 2 hours.

This elegant dish can be served as an appetizer or a dessert. It can easily be made a day or two ahead of a party. Unmold just before serving. Serve alone or with Champagne Mint Sauce (see next page) on the side.

Serves 8 to 12.

CHAMPAGNE MINT SAUCE

———

from José Gutierrez, executive chef, Chez Philippe, Peabody Hotel, Memphis, Tennessee

1 cup granulated sugar

2 cups champagne

4 pears peeled, cored and cut into small pieces

3 tablespoons water

1/3 cup mint flowers

Boil sugar and champagne together until sugar is dissolved. Add pears and simmer over a medium heat until pears are cooked, becoming almost transparent. Add water. Blend until smooth. Add mint flowers and puree until completely smooth.

This sauce was created as an accompaniment to the Champagne Fruit Terrine. It is also delicious served with roast lamb—lighter and more delicate than mint jelly—or with vanilla ice cream.

CHOCOLATE MINT ICE CREAM

———

1/2 cup mint flowers, coarsely chopped

1/4 cup granulated sugar

1/2 cup water

juice of 1/2 lemon

3 egg yolks

3 cups half-and-half

3 ounces chocolate chips

Put the mint flowers, sugar and water into a heavy saucepan over a low heat. Stir until sugar dissolves. Bring to a boil and simmer for 5 minutes. Remove from the heat and strain the syrup. Add lemon juice to the strained liquid. Beat the egg yolks until light and frothy. Slowly pour in the syrup, beating constantly. Continue to beat until the mixture thickens.

Place the half-and-half and chocolate chips in a saucepan over a low heat. Stir until the chocolate melts. Heat until the mixture is almost to the boiling point, then remove from the heat and cool the saucepan in a large bowl filled with ice cubes. Whisk the chocolate and egg mixtures together. Pour into an ice cream maker. Freeze according to manufacturer's instructions.

For a devilishly decadent presentation, serve with crème de menthe drizzled over the ice cream.

Serves 6 to 8.

MINT CHOCOLATE CAKE

2 cups granulated sugar

1-3/4 cups cake flour, sifted

3/4 cup cocoa

1-1/2 teaspoons baking soda

1 teaspoon salt

2 eggs

1 cup milk

1/2 cup vegetable oil

2 teaspoons vanilla extract

1 cup boiling water

1/3 to 1/2 cup mint flowers, coarsely chopped

butter and flour for greasing pans

confectioners' sugar

mint flowers for garnish

Preheat oven to 350°F. Mix dry ingredients together in a large bowl. In a separate bowl, mix wet ingredients. Pour wet mixture into dry, beating for 2 minutes. Add mint flowers.

Butter and flour baking pans: use a Bundt pan, two 9- or 10-inch round baking pans or a 13-by-9-inch baking pan. Pour batter into prepared pans. Bake 30 to 35 minutes or until a toothpick inserted in the center comes out clean. Cool on a wire rack 10 minutes; remove cake from pan and cool completely on wire rack.

Just before serving, dust top of cake with confectioners' sugar. Garnish with mint flowers.

Makes two 9- or 10-inch round cakes, one Bundt cake, or one 13-by-9-inch cake.

Serves 12.

PANSY

PANSY
Viola x wittrockiana
Violet family
Violaceae
Vegetal/minty flavor
Annual
Moist, rich loamy soil
Cool weather

The name pansy comes from the French *pensée* for thought or thinking of you. The flower is believed to resemble a face in deep contemplation. In Victorian times pansies codified "I think of you" in the language of flowers.

Pansies are a cheerful addition to the spring garden. Pansies are related to violets and Johnny-jump-ups, two other edible flowers. Pansies have been hybridized for over a hundred years; there are innumerable cultivars available in a wide range of colors. Commonly seen are single-colored pansies in bright hues ranging from purple, blue and deep maroon, to yellow, red, orange and white. The bicolored or tricolored pansies resemble faces and are sometimes clownlike in appearance. The flat flowers, two to five inches across, grow from six to nine inches tall.

Pansies have a slightly sweet green or grassy flavor. If you eat only the petals, the flavor is extremely mild, but if you eat the whole flower, there is a wintergreen overtone. When you eat very dark-colored pansies, your tongue turns dark—don't worry, it is temporary. Use pansies as garnishes, in fruit salads and desserts.

CULTURE

Pansies thrive in cool weather, bringing bright color to the spring garden, fading in the heat of summer, only to rebloom in the cool of autumn. Some of the newer cultivars are heat-resistant.

Pansies prefer rich, loamy, well-drained soil that is on the moist side. Grow in full sun or in light shade. Shaded soil does not dry out nearly as quickly as soil in full sun, an added benefit when gardeners are conscious of water usage.

In cold areas, start seeds indoors ten to twelve weeks before last frost date. Transplant outdoors as soon as the soil can be worked. Pansies also can be started from seed in late summer and kept over winter in a cold frame. In areas where the temperature does not go below twenty degrees Fahrenheit, pansies can be planted in fall and lightly mulched for the winter, allowing for a very early spring bloom.

Keep picking the flowers to extend the period of bloom. Pick pansies soon after the flower opens. They keep several days in the refrigerator, but are best when freshly picked.

BLACK PANSY SYRUP

———

from David Feys, co-chef, Sooke Harbour House, Sooke, British Columbia, Canada

1 cup black (or dark purple) pansy petals, loosely packed

2 cups granulated sugar, divided

1 cup water

Put pansy petals into a food processor fitted with the steel blade. Add 1/3 cup sugar. Grind pansies into sugar by pulsing 4 times, then process for about 30 seconds.

Combine sugar, pansy/sugar mixture and water in a small, nonaluminum saucepan. Over medium heat, bring the mixture to a boil. Stir once and reduce the heat to low. Allow to simmer and cook to a syrup stage. (If you have a candy thermometer, do not allow the mixture to go over 220°F.) When the mixture reaches a syrup stage, remove it from the heat and pour into a heat-proof container. Allow to cool.

The rich dark color is a wonderful contrast when poured over vanilla ice cream. This recipe was created to be served with Anise Hyssop Custard (see p. 3).

Makes about 1 cup syrup.

PINEAPPLE GUAVA

PINEAPPLE GUAVA
Feijoa sellowiana
Myrtle family
Myrtaceae
Fruity, sweet flavor
Evergreen shrub
(Zones 8–10)
Rich, well-drained soil
Full sun to light shade

I had never heard of pineapple guava before I started researching this book. Fortunately friends of mine on the West Coast told me about it—actually raved about it, saying it was one of the best-tasting flowers.

Although the common name indicates that it may be a type of guava, it is not. The flavor of the fruit is reminiscent of guava, but guava is a different genus (*Psidium*) within the myrtle family. Botanically it was named in honor of Don de Silva Feijo, a nineteenth-century botanist, and Friedrich Sellow, a German botanist and plant collector who discovered it in South America. Pineapple guava is native to southern Brazil, Paraguay, Uruguay and northern Argentina. Early in this century it was brought to California, where it is cultivated today.

The flowers appear in late spring or early summer, and are exquisite in look as well as flavor, measuring up to one and one-half inches across. The outside of the petals is white to pale pink, while the inside is deep fuchsia pink. Prominent, dark-colored stamens add to the effect of fireworks from the flowers. The petals are somewhat fleshy, and the flavor is incredible—sweet and tropical. To me it was somewhat like a freshly picked, perfectly ripe papaya or exotic melon, still warm from the sun. If you can resist picking all the flowers, the dark green fruit ripens in late autumn, with the flavor, I am told, of its name. Another bonus to this plant is its resistance to pests and to disease.

CULTURE

Pineapple guava is an evergreen shrub growing eight to ten feet tall. It responds well to pruning and can easily be maintained at a lesser height. Prune it back in the spring to keep it within bounds. The leaves are handsome—glossy dark green on top and woolly silver underneath. Use the foliage from pruned branches in flower arrangements.

In zones 8 through 10, grow it in rich, well-drained soil in a warm, sunny location. In very southern areas plant it in light shade. Mulch and protect it in late autumn as protection against fluctuating low temperatures. From zone 8 north, grow pineapple guava as a container plant outdoors in summer and bring it into a cool greenhouse for the winter.

FEIJOA FRUIT SALAD

20 seedless green grapes, cut in half

20 seedless red grapes, cut in half

2 apricots, pitted and sliced

1 peach, pitted and sliced

1 red plum, pitted and sliced

10 cherries, pitted and cut in half

2 oranges, peeled, sectioned and cut into thirds

1 kiwi, peeled and sliced

petals of 15 pineapple guava blossoms

Gently mix all ingredients together. Refrigerate in a nonmetallic bowl for several hours to allow flavors to meld. Garnish with pineapple guava petals. Refreshing served alone; elegant topped with Pineapple guava Sorbet (see below); delectable with a large dollop of Sweet Woodruff Yogurt Custard (see page 67).

Serves 4 as a luncheon course; 6 to 8 for dessert.

PINEAPPLE GUAVA SORBET

1-1/2 cups water

4 tablespoons granulated sugar

2/3 cup pineapple guava petals

2 egg whites, beaten to form soft peaks

1 tablespoon lime juice

Bring water and sugar to a boil in a small, nonaluminum saucepan. Add petals and remove saucepan from the heat.

Allow to slowly cool to room temperature. Transfer to an ice cube tray and freeze to a slush. Remove from freezer, turn into a bowl. Fold in beaten egg whites and lime juice. Return to freezer and allow to freeze.

Keeps for several weeks in the freezer, but it is unlikely that any will be left over.

Serves 4.

PINEAPPLE SAGE

PINEAPPLE SAGE
(Pineapple-scented sage)
Salvia elegans
Mint family
Lamiaceae
Sweet, minty flavor
Perennial (Zones 9–10)
Light, well-drained soil
Full sun

The leaves are opposite on the stems, dark green and rough textured. The vibrant red, one-inch tubular flowers appear in late summer and fall. The flowers are on terminal spikes that rise a foot or more above the foliage.

Pineapple sage is attractive in an annual or perennial border for the great display of color late in the season. The flowers are exquisite with the late afternoon sun shining on them, highlighting their bright red color.

The flavor of the flowers is wonderful—sweet and fruity with a hint of spice and mint.

CULTURE

Pineapple sage needs full sun. It prefers light, sandy, well-drained soil.

Plant it in the garden in the spring after all danger of frost is past. Space plants at least eighteen to twenty-four inches apart. Fertilize with an all-purpose organic fertilizer after planting.

If growing pineapple sage as a perennial, cut it back and fertilize every spring. The plant can also be divided in the spring.

Pineapple sage gets its name from the fruity fragrance of the leaves, reminiscent of the tropical pineapple.

It is a tender perennial, hardy only to zone 9. In cooler areas of the country it is usually grown as an annual. The plant, when grown as a perennial, can get up to five feet tall; when grown as an annual, it only reaches three feet in height.

LACE COOKIES

—

1-1/2 cups granulated sugar

1 cup almonds, finely chopped

3/4 cup all-purpose flour

juice of 1 orange

1/4 pound sweet (unsalted) butter, melted

1/4 cup pineapple sage flowers, coarsely chopped

Preheat oven to 400°F. In a large bowl, mix sugar, almonds and flour. Pour orange juice and melted butter into the center of the bowl. Add flowers. Stir well, mixing with a wooden spoon.

Grease a cookie sheet. Spoon a teaspoonful of batter into circles 2 inches apart. Gently flatten the cookie with a fork dipped in cold water. Bake for 5 to 7 minutes, until the cookies are lightly browned at the edges. Remove from oven and let sit 1 minute until the cookies start to firm up. Using a metal spatula, remove the cookies from the sheet before they become brittle.

Cookies can be placed over a rolling pin to form a curved shape.

Makes about 3 dozen cookies.

ʀED ʗLOVER

RED CLOVER
Trifolium pratense
Pea family
Fabaceae
Sweet flavor
Annual, self-seeding
Any garden soil

Red clover grows from six to sixteen inches tall, flowering from April to September. Upon close examination, what appears to be the one-inch pink flower reveals itself to be a densely packed head of small pealike flowers. The leaves are grouped in threes, but are narrower than most clovers, marked with a pale chevron.

Raw clover flowers are not easily digestible, especially when eaten in any quantity, but their sweet crunch is a nice addition to salad. The flowers can be dried and then brewed into a delicately flavored tea.

CULTURE

Red clover grows wild in fields and along roadsides throughout America. To some it may be considered a weed, but how lovely it is in a mass planting, gently swaying in the breeze, the honey scent of the flowers drifting toward you. You can grow it from seed—direct seed it in early to mid-spring or in late summer.

Clover is an added bonus in the garden—like most legumes, it fixes nitrogen from the air into the soil, so it helps fertilize the garden.

WARNING

Clover can cause a skin rash in some sensitive people.

In Victorian times, red clover signified industry. Although it grows wild like a native plant, red clover was an introduction from Europe. Clover cordial was a popular drink in the early days of San Francisco.

Clover was used as a food by Native Americans from coast to coast. According to Sturtevant, "Where clover is found growing wild, the Indians practice a sort of semicultivation by irrigating it and harvesting." In Ireland and Scotland, clover was also a food source. The dried flowers and seeds of white clover were ground and made into a nutritious bread.

CLOVER TEA

1/2 cup clover blossoms, fresh or dried
4 cups boiling water

Pour boiling water over clover blossoms in a teapot. Allow to steep for 5 minutes. Strain and serve.

Serves 4.

rOSE

Fossil evidence indicates that roses have existed for more than forty million years, predating man. We have been enchanted by the rose for thousands of years. The Greek poet Sappho summed it all up more than twenty-five hundred years ago when he called roses the "Queen of Flowers." In the language of flowers, roses denote love; deep red means bashful modesty; white means "I am worthy of you"; withered white rose denotes infidelity; yellow means jealousy.

There are more than two hundred species of roses and twenty thousand hybrids that man has created. The figures are not so staggering when you consider that roses were first cultivated during the Shen Nung Dynasty in China from 2737 to 2697 B.C. The Western world did not become truly enamored of the rose until the Romans cultivated them for beauty, fragrance and their purported medicinal qualities. The Romans can be credited with the first greenhouses using hot water pipes that kept these plants warm enough to bloom in winter.

As the Roman Empire declined, so did the rose. By the 1200s the church, which had looked unfavorably on roses as examples of Roman excesses, embraced the symbolism of the rose—white for the Immaculate Conception and red for Christ's blood. Rosary beads were traditionally made from a heated mixture of chopped rose petals, salt and water that was rolled to the desired shape and then strung together to form a complete rosary.

Roses are native to all areas of the world north of the equator. Although they grow perfectly well south of the equator, none are indigenous to the southern latitudes. Depending on the type of rose, hardiness varies from zones

ROSE
Rosa *spp.*
Rose family
Rosaceae
Perfumed flavor
Shrub (Zones 3–8)
Rich, well-drained soil
Full sun

3 to 8. With the myriad choices—old garden, species, rambler, climber, miniature, antique, shrub, hybrid tea, floribunda, grandiflora and miniature—roses have a place in every garden. For those without a garden, many miniatures are well suited to growing indoors under lights.

The Romans can be credited with introducing eating rose petals to Europe. This was much to the chagrin of the peasants who customarily used the rose hips. If you pick the flower, no hip will grow, as the hip is the fruit of the pollinated rose.

With all the roses to choose from, how do you pick those to eat? First, seek out *Rosa rugosa* 'alba'—the most delicious rose, with *Rosa rugosa* coming in a strong second. Many old roses are delicious. Try the Damask rose (*R. damascena*) and Apothecary rose (*R. gallica*). When choosing hybrids remember that only fragrant roses have flavorful petals. Some, however, leave a metallic aftertaste, so sample all roses before using them in the kitchen. Among my favorite modern roses are 'Tiffany,' 'Mirandy,' 'Double Delight,' 'Fragrant Cloud,' 'Perfume Delight' and 'White Lightnin.' The flavors are varied, all on the sweet side, with overtones ranging from apple to cinnamon to minty.

CULTURE

Roses need full sun. They prefer moist, rich, sandy, well-drained soil. Make sure the plants get at least one inch of water per week, more in very hot weather and when they are newly planted. If at all possible, water at ground or root level using soaker hoses or a drip-irrigation system. If you must use an above-ground sprinkler, water early in the day so that the leaves have a chance to dry and do not remain wet during the night. Proper watering techniques can reduce the incidence of blackspot and mildew in roses.

Plant roses in the spring. For bare-rooted roses or those in cardboard containers (first remove the cardboard container), soak the roses for at least six hours in tepid water. Dig a hole larger than the container the rose is in. Add to the soil removed from the hole: one-half cup bonemeal, one-half cup blood meal, two cups compost (or well-rotted manure), one-half cup organic fertilizer, one-half cup greensand and one-half cup rock phosphate. Mix well. Meanwhile, fill the hole with water to make sure it drains within fifteen minutes. If not, dig deeper, loosening more soil. Replace one-third to one-half of the amended soil into the hole, mounding to form a cone shape. Fan the roots out around the cone and hold the rose so that the bud union (large bump on the stem just above the roots) is at the proper level. (In areas with freezing winters, the union should be one to two inches below ground level. In warm areas, the union should be up to two inches above soil level.) Add soil, filling two-thirds of the hole. Add water to the top of the hole and allow it to soak in. Fill in the rest of the hole with soil, gently firming by hand. Mulch well with an organic mulch.

For roses purchased in containers, follow the directions as above, but do not soak the rose. After digging the hole and amending the soil, remove the rose from the container. Loosen some of the soil around the roots, especially if it seems potbound. Replace several inches of amended soil in the hole. Then place the rose, with the bud union at the correct level for your area. (All container grown roses have the bud union above soil level, which makes it easier for growers to ship them anywhere in the country.) Replace the rest of the amended soil, water and mulch.

Although there are many pests and diseases that can affect roses, do not be misguided into thinking that you need an array of chemical controls. I have been successfully growing roses organically for nearly twenty years. Insecticidal soap is the backbone of my regimen. I use a mixture of one tablespoon of baking soda dissolved in a gallon of water with three drops of Ivory liquid soap and spray on both sides of the leaves every four to seven days to control blackspot. I have applied milky spore to all cultivated areas (lawns and gardens) to control Japanese beetles. When I need to, I set out Japanese beetle traps thirty feet or more away from the roses or other plants to which they are attracted.

Roses are heavy feeders. My established roses each get a "spring tonic" every year, consisting of a top dressing of three cups of compost or well-rotted organic matter (manure or leaf mold), one-half cup of rock phosphate, one-half cup of bonemeal, one-half cup of blood meal and one-half cup of greensand. This is watered in with a gallon of water to which one tablespoon of Epsom salts has been added. During the growing season I give the plants a liquid foliar (leaf) feeding every two to four weeks until August (follow the package instructions for proper dilution).

In cold areas, roses need winter protection. Once the weather is steadily cold (in the forties), mound up eight or more inches of soil around the base of the rose. Once it gets cold enough for that to freeze, cover the mound with several inches of mulch. When the weather begins to warm in the spring, remove the mulch and begin to feed and prune your plants.

All roses benefit from pruning. Heavy pruning is done in the spring. Pruning is to be avoided in the fall. Always cut at a forty-five-degree angle toward an outward facing bud. Cut flowers down to the lowest five- or seven-leaflet group, again toward an outward facing leaflet. This encourages new growth outward, away from the plant, allowing for optimal air circulation. Most modern roses (climbers and tree roses are an exception) benefit from a severe pruning (down to twelve to eighteen inches) in the spring just as growth begins. Believe me, pruning is much more traumatic to you than to the plant.

It is most important that you choose the right rose for your area. Learn about the particular rose that interests you before you buy it. It may not be suited for your locale. If blackspot or mildew is a problem where you live, look for varieties that are resistant to those diseases. See what your friends and neighbors are growing successfully. Visit a local botanic garden or arboretum. You are likely to get more honest advice there than at a nursery or garden center.

WARNING

Notice that when you remove the petals from the flower, the base of the petal is whitish. Remove that part as it may be bitter.

As tempting as it may be, never accept a rose (for culinary purposes) from another garden unless you are 100 percent sure it has been grown organically.

Even with organic controls, I like to wait several days after application before harvesting roses. Wash them well before using.

ROSE PETAL SAUCE

from John Ash, culinary director, Fetzer Vineyards, Hopland, California

1/3 cup rose petals (preferably from deep red miniature varieties*)
1/2 teaspoon lemon juice
1/4 cup white wine vinegar
1/4 cup light corn syrup
1/2 cup granulated sugar
1/2 cup water
6 to 10 drops rose water (optional)

Combine first six ingredients and bring to a boil in a saucepan. Cool, add optional rose water and store in refrigerator for at least a week to develop color. Sauce may be used cold or hot drizzled on fresh fruit or ice cream.

Makes about 1 cup sauce.

* If using larger petaled varieties, gently cut petals in half or thirds.

PEAR SHERBET WITH RED CURRANT SHERBET

from Charmaine Eads, chef, Manor Farm Inn, Poulsbo, Washington

Pear sherbet:

water

3 cups granulated sugar, divided

1/3 cup pear liqueur

5 to 6 pears (Bosc or D'Anjou preferred)

1 teaspoon cinnamon

1/4 teaspoon nutmeg

1/2 cup dark-colored rose petals

Add 1 cup water and 2 cups sugar into a heavy saucepan. Bring to a boil over medium heat. Do not stir. Boil for 15 minutes. Remove from heat and allow to cool. Add pear liqueur.

Peel pears and place in a deep saucepan with enough water to cover. Add 1 cup sugar, cinnamon and nutmeg. Bring to a simmer over medium heat. Poach until pears are fork tender. Remove from heat, and remove pears from poaching liquid. Allow pears to cool.

Cut pear away from the core, discarding core. Puree pears until completely smooth. Add puree and rose petals to cooled syrup. Pour into an ice cream maker and freeze according to manufacturer's instructions. When sherbet is soft set, put in freezer.

Red currant sherbet:

water

3 cups granulated sugar, divided

1/3 cup Cassis

1-1/2 cups red currants

Add 1 cup water and 2 cups sugar into a heavy saucepan. Bring to a boil over medium heat. Do not stir. Boil for 15 minutes. Remove from heat and allow to cool. Add Cassis.

Puree currants until completely smooth. Add puree to cooled syrup. Pour into an ice cream maker and freeze according to manufacturer's instructions. When sherbet is soft set, put in freezer.

To serve, place one scoop of red currant sherbet in a dessert glass. Top with a scoop of pear sherbet. Garnish with coarsely chopped rose petals.

The sweet pear sherbet is a contrast to the tart red currant sherbet, so alternate tastes of each when eating this colorful dessert.

Serves 8.

ROSELLE

Roselle is native to the Old World tropics. It is cultivated in Florida, the Caribbean and India for its yellow flowers and fleshy calyxes. These are made into delicious jellies, sauces and a fermented beverage called roselle. Its flavor is mild with a hint of citrus.

CULTURE

Roselle is hardy to zone 10. It grows best in full sun and rich, well-drained soil. Set plants twenty-four inches apart. See Hibiscus (page 25) for detailed culture information.

ROSELLE
(Jamaican sorrel)
Hibiscus sabdariffa
Mallow family
Malvaceae
Mild flavor
Shrub (Zone 10)
Well-drained, rich soil
Full sun

ROSELLE ICE CREAM

2 cups milk
1/2 vanilla bean, split
1/2 cup roselle flowers, shredded
4 egg yolks
1/3 cup granulated sugar

Pour milk into a heavy saucepan. Add vanilla and roselle flowers. Over a medium heat, bring milk to a scald. In a large bowl, beat egg yolks with sugar until yolks become pale yellow and form a ribbonlike consistency. Gradually whisk hot milk into eggs, adding milk slowly. Continue to whisk until completely blended. Return mixture to the saucepan. Over medium heat, cook the liquid, stirring continuously until it coats a wooden spoon. Do not allow it to boil or it will curdle. Remove from heat. Cool at room temperature about 15 minutes, then refrigerate until it is well chilled. Pour into an ice cream maker and process according to manufacturer's directions.

Serves 4 to 6.

$\mathcal{S}$CENTED $\mathcal{G}$ERANIUM

SCENTED
GERANIUM
Pelargonium *spp.*
Geranium family
Geraniaceae
Floral flavor
Perennial (Zones 9–10)
Evenly moist soil
Full sun

Scented geraniums come in a range of odors and flavors, with rose geranium still the most popular and consistent. Scented geraniums are native to the Cape of Good Hope. They were first introduced into Europe in the early 1600s. It took more than a century before they made their way to America, yet by the late 1800s there were over 150 varieties described in catalogs.

In the Victorian language of flowers, lemon geranium expresses unexpected meeting while nutmeg geranium denotes expected meeting.

In their native habitat and in southern California, scented geraniums are perennial. In most of the rest of the country, they are treated as annuals or tender perennials. The leaf form is highly variable and the leaf texture can be smooth, velvety or even sticky. It is the back of the leaf that releases the scent for which each geranium is known and named. Even when they are not in bloom, it is a joy to brush your hand against the plant and smell the aroma.

There are over fifty different geraniums with a rose odor. Some can reach a height of four feet in mild areas. They bloom in June and July in indescribable hues of lavender and pink. *Pelargonium graveolens* is a large plant with lavender flowers and deeply cut, gray green leaves. It is traditionally used in rose geranium jelly and tea. *Pelargonium graveolens,* 'Lady Plymouth,' grows very large, yet is slow-growing. The leaf is deeply cut light green with a strong aroma. 'Gray Lady Plymouth' is one of the best variegated plants. It is a vigorous plant with deeply cut gray green leaves bordered with white. 'Rober's Lemon Rose' has one of the sweetest rose scents and flavors. The leaf is long and thick, resembling a tomato leaf. *Pelargonium capitatum* 'Attar of Roses' is considered by many the best of the rose-scented geraniums. Its three-lobed, crenated leaves are light green, soft and hairy and the flowers are lavender. *Pelargonium denticulatum* has finely cut leaves growing densely on a compact plant.

Lemon geranium leaves are usually flatter, with edges more toothed than rose geraniums. They also bloom in June and July, often with pink flowers. *Pelargonium crispum* is one of the finest lemon-scented geraniums. The leaves are small, fluted and ruffled, growing on upright stems. The flowers are orchid pink. With its treelike shape, it makes an excellent container plant. *Pelargonium crispum* 'Prince Rupert' with its strong lemon scent, can easily grow into a small shrub in a good growing season. *Pelargonium crispum* 'Prince Rupert Variegated' has ruffled green leaves variegated with a creamy white. The scent is milder than 'Prince Rupert', and it is not nearly so vigorous. *Pelargonium limoneum* 'Lady Mary' has fan-shaped toothed leaves and bears magenta flowers in summer.

Pelargonium fragrans 'Nutmeg' has a strong scent. It creeps, making it excellent at the edge of a border or in a planter allowed to trail down the sides. The leaves are small and grayish green.

The flowers of the scented geraniums are mild-flavored versions of the scent of the leaf. The recipes that follow call for rose geranium, but you can substitute any flavor you like.

CULTURE

Scented geraniums are well suited for growing in containers, but can also be planted in the ground. They thrive in sunny locations in evenly moist soil. They are not grown from seed, rather from rooted cuttings. They are available commercially, or you can share cuttings with friends. The popularity of scented geraniums is rapidly growing. Even the smallest nurseries can be relied on to carry several different varieties.

Plant scented geraniums in containers at least five inches deep—double that is preferable. Use a mixture of one part Perlite, one part well-rotted compost or garden loam and one part peat moss for potting them. Feed every two to three weeks.

Scented geraniums are frost tender. Remove any leaves as they yellow. Bring the plants indoors before frost to winter over in pots, or simply treat them as annuals and allow them to die in the garden. The entire plant can be brought in, or if space does not allow, take cuttings and root them. When you bring them indoors, place them in the sunniest location possible.

WARNING

Do not eat the 'Citronella' scented geranium, which is being touted as a mosquito and bug repellent, although it has yet to prove itself to me. In general, if the leaf does not have an appetizing aroma, do not eat the flowers.

ROSE GERANIUM JELLY

1 pint apple jelly

1/2 cup rose geranium petals

Heat the apple jelly over a low heat until it turns liquid. Add the rose geranium petals and stir. Remove from heat and pour jelly into a jelly glass. Allow to cool. Cover and refrigerate. Delicious heated and drizzled over vanilla ice cream or plain pound cake. Use within 2 weeks.

ROSE ANGEL CAKE

———

1 angel food cake, cut into 3 equal layers
orange juice
Rose Geranium Jelly (see page 57)
vanilla ice cream, softened

Place the first layer of the angel food cake in an angel food cake (tube) pan. Lightly sprinkle the layer with orange juice. Spread a thin layer of Rose Geranium Jelly over the cake. Place the next layer atop the first. Sprinkle lightly with orange juice and spread thickly with ice cream. Add the last layer of cake. Sprinkle lightly with orange juice and spread with Rose Geranium Jelly. Spread with ice cream. Put cake in freezer until ice cream hardens.

Remove from freezer and gently unmold onto a serving plate. Spread ice cream over the entire cake and return to freezer until ice cream hardens.

Serve garnished with rose geranium petals.

Serves 10 to 16.

SCENTED GERANIUM ICE CREAM

———

from James O'Shea, chef, West Street Grill, Litchfield, Connecticut

5 to 7 scented geranium leaves (rose, lime or nutmeg),
  roughly chopped
2 teaspoons scented geranium petals (same scent as leaves)
1-1/4 cups half-and-half
1/2 cup granulated sugar
4 egg yolks
1 cup heavy cream

Combine leaves, petals and half-and-half in a small saucepan. Bring to a boil. Remove from heat and allow to cool for 20 minutes.

In a small stainless steel saucepan whisk together sugar and egg yolks. Continue to whisk until mixture is light and frothy. Slowly whisk in half-and-half. Cook over a low heat, stirring continually, until custard coats the back of a wooden spoon. Strain custard into a bowl and set into an ice bath to cool.

Beat heavy cream until it forms peaks. Gently fold cream into the cooled custard. Freeze in an ice cream maker according to manufacturer's instructions. Remove from ice cream maker and place in freezer overnight to set.

Serve in small glasses garnished with additional scented geranium leaves and petals.

Serves 4 to 6.

ROSE GERANIUM CAKE

2-2/3 cup cake flour

1 tablespoon baking powder

1 teaspoon salt

2/3 cup shortening

1-1/4 cups granulated sugar

1 cup milk

1 teaspoon vanilla

5 egg whites

1/2 cup granulated sugar

2/3 cup rose geranium petals, coarsely chopped

1 cup pecans, chopped

confectioners' sugar for decoration

rose geranium petals for garnish

Preheat oven to 375°F. Sift flour once, then measure. Sift together with the baking powder and salt three times.

In a separate bowl, cream shortening. Add 1-1/4 cups of sugar gradually, creaming until mixture is light and fluffy. Add flour and milk alternately to creamed sugar, beating with each addition until smooth. Add vanilla and blend.

In a separate bowl, beat egg whites until they are foamy. Gradually add in 1/2 cup sugar, beating until mixture forms soft peaks.

Fold egg white mixture into batter. Add rose geranium petals and pecans and mix well. Pour batter into a buttered and floured 13-by-9-inch baking pan (or use a Bundt pan). Bake for about 35 to 45 minutes or until a toothpick inserted in the center comes out clean.

Take cake out of the oven and cool it on a wire rack for 10 minutes. Remove the cake from the pan and leave on the rack until completely cooled. Decorate with sifted confectioners' sugar and additional rose geranium petals.

Serves 18 to 24.

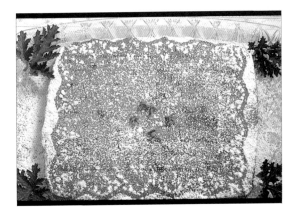

ƒIGNET MARIGOLD

SIGNET
MARIGOLD
(Dwarf marigold)
Tagetes signata
(T. tenuifolia)
Composite family
Asteraceae
Spicy, herbal flavor
Annual
Moist, well-drained
soil
Full sun

Gem' has dainty, one-half–inch lemon-yellow flowers; 'Tangerine Gem' has vibrant one-half–inch orange blooms.

The flavor of the signets is the best of any marigolds, almost like a spicy tarragon. Remove the white part from the end of the petal where it was attached to the flower as it is very bitter.

I have tasted other marigolds over the years, and the flavor of some is actually repugnant. If you absolutely must eat a large, double marigold, I suggest trying one of the Inca series—either yellow or orange. The flavor is tangy to bitter, also with a tarragon overtone.

Marigold petals can be dried for use in the winter. Follow the same instructions as for calendula.

CULTURE

Marigolds prefer full sun and moist, well-drained, moderately fertile soil.

Marigolds are easily grown from seed. Start the seed indoors six weeks before the last frost date, or direct seed them into the garden after danger of frost is past. Allow six to eight inches between plants.

Marigolds are somewhat tolerant to drought, but they do need occasional water, especially when the plants are young. Keep picking the flowers and they will bloom all through the summer and up until frost.

WARNING

Marigolds may be harmful in large amounts. Eat them occasionally and in moderation.

Marigolds are annuals, native from New Mexico to Argentina. Signet marigolds are related to the popular African and French marigold (which, contrary to their names, are from Central and South America). In the Victorian language of flowers, marigolds signify jealousy.

Marigolds have finely dissected, strongly scented leaves. The signet marigolds grow to form compact, ten- to twelve-inch rounded mounds. Even before the flowers open the foliage is an attractive green that looks almost like a fern. The scent of the foliage is much better than that of other marigolds; when bruised it has a lemon scent.

The signet marigolds bear diminutive, single flowers no more than one-half to one inch in diameter. 'Lemon

MARIGOLD BUTTER

——

petals from 20 single marigolds
1/2 pound butter, softened to room temperature

Finely chop the petals. Mix them into the softened butter. Let sit at cool room temperature several hours. Roll into a log shape using waxed paper. Refrigerate overnight. Keeps refrigerated up to 2 weeks, frozen up to 6 months. Cut slices to garnish any grilled fish dish, or serve on Morning Sunshine Muffins (below).

MORNING SUNSHINE MUFFINS

——

1-3/4 cups all-purpose flour
2 teaspoons double-acting baking powder
1/2 teaspoon salt
1/4 cup granulated sugar
2 eggs
2 tablespoons melted butter
3/4 cup milk
3/4 cup chopped dates
2 tablespoons marigold petals, chopped

Preheat oven to 425°F. Sift together flour, baking powder, salt and sugar. In a separate bowl beat eggs. Mix in butter, milk, dates and marigold petals. Add wet ingredients to dry, mixing just enough to evenly moisten. Spoon mixture into greased muffin tins, filling halfway. Bake for 15 to 20 minutes, or until tops are lightly browned. Delicious served with marigold butter.

Makes 12 muffins.

$QUASH $LOSSOMS

SQUASH
BLOSSOMS
Curcubita pepo *spp.*
Gourd family
Curcubitaceae
Vegetal flavor
Annual
Enriched soil
Full sun

Native Americans grew summer and winter squash long before the Spanish brought other varieties to America. Indians used the male blossoms in a number of ways from side dishes to desserts. The flowers of numerous varieties of both summer and winter squash can be eaten, yet the most commonly consumed is the zucchini flower.

All squash are tender annuals. In general, they are vining plants and can grow to prodigious lengths, meandering through the garden. Newer bush-type varieties of some squash have been introduced, but even they take up at least three feet square, if not more. Varieties that produce smallish fruit can be trained on a trellis. Be sure that the squash, once formed, are supported.

In general squash leaves are large and attractive. The vining types are excellent to grow on a sunny hillside. There they can run as much as they want, while providing needed erosion control and ground cover. The bush varieties are handsome in a perennial border or in a large container.

The flowers vary in size, but can get up to four inches across when fully opened. Most flowers are one to three inches deep—perfect for stuffing. Squash flowers are most often a vibrant yellow, but may be pale yellow or yellow-orange.

Some cooks prefer to use male blossoms, others female. It is easy to tell the difference. Male flowers are on long, slender stems. Female flowers are short-stemmed. Look closely and you can see the miniature squash behind the female flower. If the female is not pollinated, the flower and the little squash turn brown and fall off.

Using female flowers is one of the best ways to practice squash birth control. If you have grown zucchini, you know how the cute little four-inch squash can turn, seemingly overnight, into a baseball bat in both size and texture. You do need the males to pollinate the females. It can be attractive to have both the squash and the flower in a recipe.

The flavor of squash blossoms is best described as mildly vegetal.

CULTURE

Squash grow best in full sun. Summer squash grow so quickly it is easiest to direct seed them into the garden once all danger of frost is past. Squash that need a long growing season should be started indoors in the coldest areas.

To meet squash's heavy nutrient needs, dig a hole about a foot deep and fill it with well-rotted manure or compost. Form a hill with the soil from the hole. Plant two or three seeds in the hole. Water well throughout the growing season.

Black plastic mulch helps to warm the soil early in the season and keep out weeds. Do not use black plastic in warm climates. In warm areas, it pays to mulch, but choose an organic material such as grass clippings, hay, pine needles or cocoa hulls.

Squash are susceptible to vine borer, squash beetle and squash bug. To prevent infestation, cover the squash as soon as they germinate with spun/bonded material such as Agronet or Reemay. Remove the material once the plants begin to flower or they will not get pollinated.

Mildew can be a problem, usually later in the season. At that point, it is best to simply rip the plant out, especially if it has already produced squash.

When buying seeds or plants, I look for modern hybrid varieties that are labeled as disease-resistant. I have also found that some of the heirloom varieties, by virtue of the fact that they have been around for so long, perform well, are disease-resistant and are more flavorful than the newer hybrids.

HAVASUPAI INDIAN SQUASH BLOSSOM PUDDING

kernels from 3 ears of green corn
water
2 to 3 cups squash blossoms, destemmed
salt

Place green corn kernels in a saucepan. Add just enough water to cover corn. Cook over medium-low heat for half an hour. In another saucepan, place squash blossoms. Cover with water and bring to a boil. Cook until tender. Drain blossoms, and mash. Stir mashed blossoms into green corn and continue to cook until thickened. Season to taste with salt.

Serves 4.

SUNFLOWER

SUNFLOWER

Helianthus annuus

Composite family

Asteraceae

Bittersweet flavor

Annual

Well-drained soil

Full sun

The Aztecs worshipped this giant of flowers as a symbol of the sun. Indeed, the shape and brilliance of this annual is like the sun. It can grow a prodigious ten feet tall, with flowers measuring twelve inches or more across in cultivation. In the wild, the flower becomes more diminutive in size, but is still impressive.

The sunflower was one of the flowers chosen as an almost perfect model of design for modern art by the Aesthetic Movement. In the Victorian language of flowers, the sunflower stands for false riches.

Wild sunflowers, the diminutive parent of the domesticated giant, grow in the prairies and roadsides from Minnesota to Texas. In other areas sunflowers simply escaped from cultivation. Native Americans cultivated the sunflower for several thousand years. In Arizona the Hopi and Havasupai Indians developed hybrid strains several hundred years ago. In fact, the sunflower is the only major crop that originated in the lower forty-eight states. The sunflower was introduced from America to Europe in the late 1500s. Today the Russians are the largest producer of sunflower seeds, having developed most of the cultivars we now grow in America.

The broad, heart-shaped leaves are rough and somewhat hairy. Large flower heads consist of twenty to twenty-five showy yellow-orange ray flowers surrounding a yellow, brown or purple-brown central disk. The flowers bloom in midsummer and continue into early fall. The flat seeds develop from the disk flowers and are a delicacy to birds, animals and humans. It is often a challenge to harvest seeds in your own garden for your enjoyment. Sometimes it is best to get your enjoyment from watching the creatures that come to feed from this magnificent plant.

The flower is best eaten in the bud stage when it tastes similar to artichokes. Once the flower opens, the petals may be used like chrysanthemums, the flavor is distinctly bittersweet.

CULTURE

Sunflowers grow best in full sun. They prefer well-drained, friable soil of almost any type. The looser the soil, the deeper the roots can establish themselves.

Sunflowers can get unwieldy in the garden, often toppling after heavy winds or rains. Staking will help only if the stakes are deep enough in the ground. Protect tall varieties by planting in a sheltered location. Sun-flowers make a lovely screen to hide an ugly wall or fence. 'Sunspot' is a dwarf variety growing only two feet tall, yet bearing full-sized flowers that are perfect for the front of a flower border.

Sunflowers grow quickly from seed. Plant seeds one inch deep or more in the ground two weeks after the last spring frost date. Allow ten to fifteen inches between plants.

WARNING

The pollen can cause allergic reactions in sensitive individuals.

SUNBUDS

8 *sunflower buds*
2 *tablespoons butter*
3 *tablespoons plain bread crumbs*
juice of 2 medium lemons
confectioners' sugar

Bring a pot of water to a boil. Add sunflower buds. Boil for 2 minutes. While water is boiling, bring a second pot of water to a boil. After the sunflower buds have cooked for 3 minutes, transfer them to the second pot of water. Discard the first pot of water. This gets rid of any bitterness. Continue to cook buds until fork tender. Drain and set aside.

In a skillet, melt the butter. Add bread crumbs and stir, sautéing lightly. When bread crumbs turn golden, toss in sunflower buds. Pour on lemon juice to taste, toss to coat. Sprinkle generously with confectioners' sugar. Serve immediately. Garnish, if desired, with sunflower petals.

Serves 4.

SWEET WOODRUFF

SWEET
WOODRUFF
Galium odoratum
Madder family
Rubiaceae
Sweet flavor
Perennial (Zones 5—8)
Well-drained, rich soil
Partial to full shade

Sweet woodruff is sometimes seen listed as *Asperula odorata*. It is a fragrant, low-growing perennial herb. More often than not, it is grown for its ornamental properties—as a shade-tolerant ground cover—than for any herbal properties.

"Wood" in the common name refers to the fact that sweet woodruff grows wild deep in the dark woods. "Ruff" comes from the French *rovelle*, meaning wheel, relating to the arrangement of the leaves around the stem.

Traditionally sweet woodruff has been used as an aromatic ingredient in May wine. Often a sprig of sweet woodruff is placed in a glass of wine in spring. Germans drink May wine as a spring tonic as well as to greet the season.

Native to Europe and Eurasia, sweet woodruff has become naturalized in some areas of America. Growing up to twelve inches high, it makes an ideal ground cover. The leaves are deep green in whorls of six to eight around the square stem. In mid-spring small, white, funnel-shaped flowers appear in loose clusters.

The flowers are sweet smelling and tasting with a nutty, vanilla flavor. The foliage has no scent when freshly picked, but soon the sweet aroma of newly mown hay appears. The smell intensifies as the plant dries. For this reason, it was often strewn in homes and churches to freshen rooms.

CULTURE

Sweet woodruff can grow in almost any type of soil, but prefers well-drained, rich soil. It is a perfect choice for shade, performing equally well in partial to full shade.

You can grow sweet woodruff from seed, but it is slow to germinate. It is much easier to divide existing clumps to create new plants. Once established, it will self-seed. Since it also spreads by underground runners, sweet woodruff can become somewhat invasive. If you find it is, dig some up and share it with friends.

WARNING

Sweet woodruff can have a blood-thinning effect in large amounts. Anyone taking coumarin should avoid eating the flowers.

MAY WINE

1 gallon dry white wine

10 sprigs sweet woodruff with leaves, coarsely chopped

4 tablespoons granulated sugar

1 bottle (32 ounces) ginger ale

12 fresh strawberries

12 sprigs sweet woodruff with flowers

In a large bowl, mix 4 cups of wine with the chopped sweet woodruff. Stir occasionally and let sit for at least 12 hours. Strain and remove the woodruff. Add sugar and mix well. Pour in remaining wine and ginger ale. Stir to blend liquids. Serve with a sprig of sweet woodruff and a strawberry in a tall wineglass.

For a more festive drink, substitute champagne for the ginger ale. Cheers!

Serves 12.

SWEET WOODRUFF ICE CREAM

6 sprigs of sweet woodruff (leaves and flowers)

2 cups half-and-half (for a very rich dessert, use heavy cream, less rich, use milk)

2 egg yolks

2 teaspoons honey

Put the sweet woodruff and half-and-half in a heavy saucepan over a low heat. Cover and heat until it almost comes to a boil (10 to 15 minutes). Remove from the heat and strain the liquid. Beat the egg yolks and honey until frothy. Add the half-and-half in a steady stream, beating continuously. Continue to beat the mixture into a light froth. Pour the mixture into an ice cream machine and process according to manu-facturer's instructions. Serve before it freezes completely hard. It will keep several months in the freezer.

Serves 6.

SWEET WOODRUFF YOGURT CUSTARD

1 cup plain yogurt

1 tablespoon honey

2 egg yolks

6 sprigs sweet woodruff (with flowers)

Whisk the yogurt, honey and egg yolks until frothy. Pour into the top of a double boiler over low heat. Add the sweet woodruff. Cover and let cook slowly for 10 minutes, stirring occasionally. Remove the sweet woodruff and discard. Continue to cook over low heat, stirring constantly as custard thickens. This can take up to 20 minutes. When thickened, remove from heat. Serve hot, at room temperature or chilled.

Serves 4.

TUBEROUS BEGONIA

TUBEROUS BEGONIA
(Hybrid tuberous begonia)
Begonia x tuberhybrida
Begonia family
Begoniaceae
Citrus flavor
Tuber (Zone 10)
Moist, fertile soil
Partial to full shade

Begonias are named for Michel Begon, a French patron of botany. Hybrid tuberous begonias, as their name implies, are a human-made hybrid, created from crosses between seven different species of begonia. The first hybrids appeared in the early 1870s. The British were trying to achieve great numbers of flowers on the plants coupled with variations of colors. At the same time the French were creating double-flowered varieties. In 1875, John Laing, a well-known British hybridizer, got the best of the British and Continental hybrids and started his own breeding program, which ultimately surpassed both of his sources. Even though they were new on the scene, tuberous begonias found their way into the Victorian language of flowers, signifying deformity.

As their name also implies, these begonias are bulblike, growing from tubers. Tuberous begonias grow up to eight-een inches tall, with upright or spreading habits. The stems are fleshy (and edible). Leaves vary in color and shape, and are often somewhat wrinkled in appearance. Tuberous begonias are often grown as container plants. Some with pendulous flowers, especially lend themselves to growing in hanging baskets.

This plant is grown for its large (up to four inches), showy, waxy flowers that bloom in summer. The colors range through white, yellow, orange, pink, red and combinations. The flowers come in different shapes, leading to the classification as rose, carnation, camellia, ruffled or picotee. The flowers are usually in groups of three, with two smaller female flowers surrounding the larger, central male flower.

The flower has no scent to give any clue to its flavor. Surprisingly the flower has a tangy citrus taste. This is due in part to the oxalic acid in the petals.

CULTURE

In zone 10, tuberous begonias can be grown and kept outdoors year round. They prefer partial to full shade. In spring, plant them in moist, fertile, well-drained soil. Mulch them well to keep the soil cool and moist. In fall, dig up the bulbs after the foliage has been browned out by frost. Store the bulbs in a cool, dry place over the winter.

In all other areas, treat tuberous begonias as tender bulbs. In late winter, place the tubers on top of a shallow pan of soilless mix (moistened peat works well). They grow best at a temperature of sixty-five degrees Fahrenheit. I place the pan on a moist heating pad set to low. (Only use the type of heating pad that specifies moist and dry heat, or you can run into major electrical problems.) This gives excellent bottom heat. At the first signs of life, they are potted up, using a soilless potting medium. Keep them in bright light, but avoid direct sun. Once all danger of frost has passed, move them outside into a cool area in partial to full shade. Bring the plants indoors in the fall. Stop watering. Once the stems wither, pull them off. Store the tubers in a cool dry place in a mixture of peat and sand.

WARNING
The petals contain oxalic acid. Eat them in moderation. Do not eat petals from any other begonias. Only hybrid tuberous begonia flowers are edible.

PEACHY KEEN BEGONIAS

1 pint plain yogurt
2 peaches, pureed *
tuberous begonia petals

Mix yogurt and peach puree together in a nonmetallic bowl. Refrigerate at least 2 hours. Serve as a dip, garnished with a whole begonia flower surrounded by begonia petals.

Serves 1 to 10, depending on how much yogurt they dip and eat.

*The easiest way to puree a ripe peach is to run it over a grater—instant puree without a lot of dishes to wash.

VIOLET

VIOLET

(English violet, sweet violet, sweet-scented violet, blue violet)

Viola odorata

Violet family

Violaceae

Perfumed flavor

Perennial (Zones 6–9)

Moist well-drained soil

Sun to shade

The ancient Greeks and Romans looked to violets to help cure some of their ills, from insomnia and gout to headaches and even to calm anger. Violets mean different things in the Victorian language of flowers depending on the color of the flower. Blue for faithfulness, purple signifies ever in my mind, white means modesty and yellow denotes rural happiness.

Although violets are native to North Africa, Europe and Asia, they have now become naturalized throughout most of North America. Violets have been cultivated for more than two thousand years. They are related to pansies and Johnny-jump-ups, two other edible flowers.

Sweet violets are creeping perennials that bloom in early spring. The dark green, heart-shaped leaves grow low to the ground in rosettes. The plant is only about six inches tall. Flowers are sweetly scented, appearing singly on long stalks. Flowers range in color from deep violet to rose, white and mottled white.

The flavor of the sweet violet is sweet and perfumed. The slightly tart leaves are a delicious salad accompaniment. Violets go well with fruit, desserts and salads. The flowers can be steeped to make a delightfully fragrant tea. Candied violets are an old-fashioned decoration for wedding cakes.

CULTURE

Violets grow best in partial shade. They will grow happily in poor soil, yet will thrive in a well-fertilized lawn. For best results, plant them in fertile, moist, well-drained soil rich in organic matter. To some, violets are second only to dandelions as a spring lawn weed.

Violets spread by rooting runners called stolons. The easiest way to cultivate violets is to dig up one or more clumps from an existing area and transplant wherever you want them. If you do not have violets in your garden, you can probably find some growing at friends, neighbors or relatives. They will probably be more than happy to share some with you. You can transplant violets in spring or fall.

Violets can be grown from seed. Place the seeds in the refrigerator for several days. This is called stratifying. Then sow the seeds outdoors in the spring or start them indoors eight to ten weeks before the last frost date in spring. Violet seeds need darkness to germinate, so cover outdoor seeds with enough soil to eliminate light. Indoor seeds can be placed in a closet until germination takes place. Seeds take from one to three weeks to germinate. Transplant seedlings outdoors around the last frost date. Allow five to eight inches between plants.

VIOLET LAVENDER SORBET

———

1-1/2 cups water, divided

3/4 cup granulated sugar, divided

1/4 cup lavender flowers

1/2 cup violets

2 tablespoons lime juice

Pour 1 cup water into a saucepan. Add 1/2 cup sugar. Bring to a boil and continue to cook for 4 minutes. Remove from heat and allow the syrup to cool to room temperature.

Fit a food processor with the metal chopping blade. Add lavender flowers and 1/4 cup sugar to the bowl. Process for 3 minutes, or until the flowers and sugar are completely blended and in tiny pieces. Add the processed mixture to the cooled syrup and stir well. Allow to stand for 1 hour at room temperature. Strain to remove any particles. Set strained syrup aside.

Bring 1/2 cup water to a boil in a nonmetallic saucepan. Remove from heat and add violets. Allow to steep for 15 minutes, stirring occasionally. Strain through a piece of cheesecloth. Squeeze cheesecloth tightly to release the blue color.

Blend the lavender syrup with the violet infusion. Add lime juice. Freeze in an ice cream maker according to manufacturer's instructions.

Serves 4 to 6.

ORANGES WITH VIOLET SYRUP

———

Syrup:

1 cup water

3 cups granulated sugar

1-1/2 cup violets

3 oranges

In a nonaluminum saucepan, boil all ingredients for 10 minutes or until thickened into a syrup. Strain through cheesecloth into a clean glass jar. Seal and store in the refrigerator for up to 2 weeks.

Darker colored flowers yield a darker syrup.

Slice 3 oranges and cut in half. Arrange the slices on plates and drizzle with violet syrup. Garnish, if desired, with candied violets.

CHOCOLATE VIOLET CAKE

2 cups cake flour

1/2 cup unsweetened cocoa

2-1/2 teaspoons baking powder

1 teaspoon salt

1-1/3 cups violet sugar

3/4 cup butter

3 eggs

1 teaspoon vanilla extract

1/2 cup milk

Preheat oven to 350°F. Sift together flour, cocoa, baking powder and salt in a bowl. Set aside. Cream together violet sugar and butter in a large bowl. Add 1 egg, continue to beat until light and fluffy. Add remaining eggs, beating after each addition. Add vanilla. Alternate adding flour mixture and milk into creamed butter mixture, gently folding to mix ingredients.

Lightly grease and flour two 9-inch cake pans. Divide batter between the two pans. Bake about 20 to 25 minutes. When done, top will spring back when gently pressed and tooth-pick inserted into center of cake comes out clean. Remove from oven and cool pans on a wire rack for 10 minutes. Gently remove cakes from pans, and cool completely on wire rack.

Decorate with your favorite icing (either chocolate or vanilla is good on this cake), or simply dust with confectioners' sugar. Candied violets add the finishing touch to this sinful dessert.

Serves 10 to 12.

EDIBLE FLOWERS IN THE GARDEN

WHAT IS SAFE, WHAT IS NOT— TOXIC FLOWERS

The history of edible flowers dates back thousands of years to the Chinese as well as Greek and Roman cultures. Yet all flowers are not edible; some are poisonous. While the main thrust of this book is promoting the edibility of flowers, it is equally important to know which flowers should not be eaten under any circumstances.

In a way, flowers can be compared to wild mushrooms. Many are truly culinary delights, some have little flavor, others taste bad and a few are poisonous. I certainly do not want to frighten anyone. Only a few flowers are as deadly as poisonous mushrooms, yet the point needs to be made that some flowers can cause unpleasant side effects and should not be eaten.

Certain chemicals are more concentrated in the flower—those responsible for scent and, in some cases, those responsible for flavor. In some cases the toxicity of the plant is concentrated in the flower.

As the popularity of edible flowers has grown, so has the inappropriate use of flowers. I tend to see things in black and white. Anything that is on a plate of food, whether it is an individual plate or a serving platter, should be edible. That is not always the case. Over the years I have seen toxic flowers used to decorate wedding cakes and put on plates as garnishes. In each case

I made a point of speaking to whomever is responsible for the food.

Often the people responded that the flowers were from their own gardens and were grown organically. I suppose we should be grateful that at least the idea of using only organically grown flowers on food has managed to sink into people's consciousness. Unfortunately, usually the next words out of their mouths were, "Well, we didn't expect anyone to eat it. It's just to look pretty."

To my way of thinking, if you want the table or presentation to look pretty, arrange flowers in a vase. If they are on a plate, they should be edible. Not enough studies have been done on the toxicity of plants to know how much is toxic. Is the plant so toxic that several drops of sap from a cut stem on a wedding cake could cause stomach distress or worse? Toxicity not only varies from plant to plant, but what affects one person might not affect another. Perhaps I, as a healthy, active adult who is on no medication, could tolerate eating a potentially toxic petal with no untoward side effects. Give that same petal to a two-year-old child who only weighs thirty pounds, and the results might be very different. Or give the same petal to an eighty-five-year-old woman with high blood pressure and heart problems who is on a variety of medications. Once again, the results could be quite different.

In an attempt to help you discern what is safe to eat and what is not, I include an extensive list of toxic plants at the end of this chapter. You may have noticed that this chapter has no photographs. This was a purposeful decision on my part. Every flower that is shown in this book is edible. The individual identification photographs for each plant are large enough so that, coupled with the written description, you can positively identify a flower as edible before it passes your lips. If you are at all uncertain of a flower's identity, play it safe and do not eat it. There is no way to tell just by looking at a plant whether it is edible, nontoxic or toxic; that is, unless you are looking at it with a keen eye and a good reference book that not only gives clear photographs (or color illustrations) of the plant, but also a description of it.

IT'S ALL IN A NAME

The flowers that are included in this book as safe and edible have been extensively researched. Some of them have warnings about amounts that are safe to eat and possible allergic reactions. A number of flowers that have been listed in other books or articles as edible are not included in this book. That is because I could not find sufficient (or any) reliable documentation of their edibility.

I had to reject, out of hand, any source that used only common names. Common names vary too much from one locale to another, and certainly from one country to another. Botanic names had to check out. As I delved deeper, I sometimes discovered why a particular plant suddenly appeared on or disappeared from an edible flower list. Often it boiled down to common names—two or more totally disparate plants had the same (or similar) common name. Which one has the edible flowers? Only a check of botanic names can sort all this out.

IF IT'S NOT TOXIC IT MUST BE EDIBLE—WRONG

If a plant is not listed on the toxic list, is it edible? Definitely not. First of all, the list of toxic plants at the end of the chapter is by no means definitive. It includes some of the more commonly known and grown plants in the United States.

For a flower to be considered edible, there should be something more enticing than the fact that it is not toxic. Certainly appearances count when it comes to flowers, but the biggest consideration is flavor. All the edible flowers have flavors that are identifiable to the palate. Not everyone has the same tastes in food or flowers. Some people like sweets; they are likely to be drawn to the sweet flowers. Other people enjoy spicy or piquant food; the spicy and bitter flowers may be more to their liking. Yet despite the range and intensity of flavors, all the flowers included are palatable.

Not enough research has been done on the edibility and/or toxicity of plants in general, not to mention plant parts like flowers. It would be foolhardy to go into the garden and sample flowers that might be considered safe because they are not on the toxic list. Let me repeat, the list is by no means complete. Perhaps that flower is attractive, and the color is lovely, but what else is known about it? Perhaps there is a chemical in the petals that acts as an abortifactant (causes spontaneous abortion)—unless you were pregnant, who would know? Let's examine toxicity in a bit more detail.

PLANT TOXINS

There has been poor documentation of plant poisoning; even less exists specific to flower poisoning. To further muddle the issue there has been a lack of adequate research on the chemical makeup of plants. So many questions have yet to be answered concerning plant toxicity. The very nature of plants and their complexity only confounds the problem.

Within a single plant species the degree of toxicity may vary depending on where in the world the plant is grown. The variables are many and diverse: soil type, moisture content, amount of sunlight and the age of the plant, to name a few. One plant can have hundreds of chemical compounds in varying amounts. It is a monumental task for a well-funded researcher to determine which substances and at what levels of concentration cause toxic effects. That is without the variable mentioned earlier in the chapter—the person who is ingesting the plant. If the material is ingested on an empty stomach, logic tells us that the effect will be different than if it were eaten after a large meal. How do the chemicals in the plant interact with all the other foodstuffs? Or with the aspirin, cold pill, antibiotic or diuretic that was taken at the same time, one hour ago, two hours ago, etc.?

To confound the issue, a plant may contain toxic substances and not cause poisoning. The toxins must be present in high enough concentrations that are then assimilated to cause poisoning. So chemical analysis alone may not indicate whether or not a plant is toxic.

A great deal of what we know about toxicity and plants comes from reports of farmers on reactions that livestock have had to plants. Unfortunately our digestive system is much different from that of a cow or horse—cat or dog for that matter. Laboratory research with mice (which are strikingly similar to man in so many ways that they have become vital to medical research) has helped determine the potential toxicity of many plants.

There are many ways plants cause poisoning. Nontoxic and even edible plants accumulate substances from the soil, including pesticides. Some plants contain small amounts of toxic substances. Spinach and tuberous begonia flowers contain some oxalic acid. Only when they are eaten in abundance does this pose a threat.

Poisoning in humans is usually the result of eating plants that contain toxic substances that are a natural part of them. Little is known about why plants produce toxic substances. Some may simply be a waste product of plant metabolism. Others may have a function in plant maintenance: some toxins act as natural insecticides, keeping potential predators at bay.

The types of plant toxins are widely varied. Science has only discovered the tip of the iceberg of the chemical nature of plants and animals. The most frequently found toxins in plants are alkaloids. They are complex organic compounds, like nicotine in tobacco and the many alkaloids in marijuana that cause a drug effect. Another group of toxins are glycosides, which are poisonous carbohydrates. Cyanogenetic glycosides, for example, give off cyanide (a very poisonous substance) as a by-product. Digitalis (foxglove) contains cardiac glycosides that affect the heartbeat, which in therapeutic dosages is a valuable medical tool. Many other plant substances, including resins, acids (let's not forget oxalic acid) and amines can cause toxicity.

TOXIC EFFECTS

The toxic effects, as demonstrated from all the information above, of ingesting a "poisonous" plant can be quite variable.

Effects may be slight—mild irritation of the mouth, sneezing, or a little heartburn. They can be moderate—burning feeling in the mouth and throat, nausea, upset stomach, diarrhea or cramping. Even more pronounced effects demand immediate medical attention (call your local poison control center)—sweating, rapid breathing or difficulty breathing, rapid or slow heartbeat, vomiting, unconsciousness, numbness or tingling in the extremities. If there is any toxic reaction to eating a flower, especially if it is immediate—get medical attention. Bring the plant along for more accurate diagnosis.

For the last time—IF YOU CANNOT POSITIVELY IDENTIFY A FLOWER AS EDIBLE, DO NOT EAT IT.

POISONOUS PLANTS AND FLOWERS—A BRIEF LIST

COMMON NAME	BOTANIC NAME
Aconite (wolfsbane, monkhood)	*Aconitum* spp.
Anemone (windflower)	*Anemone* spp.
Anthurium	*Anthurium* spp.
Atamasco lily	*Zephyranthes* spp.
Autumn crocus	*Colchicum autumnale*
Azalea	*Azalea* spp. (*Rhododendron* spp.)
Baneberry	*Actaea* spp.
Black locust	*Robinia pseudo-acacia*
Bloodroot	*Sanguinaria canadensis*
Boxwood	*Buxus* spp.
Burning bush (strawberry bush, spindle tree, wahoo)	*Euonymus* spp.
Buttercup	*Ranunculus* spp.
Butterfly weed	*Asclepias* spp.
Caladium	*Caladium* spp.
Calla (calla lily)	*Calla palustris* (*Zantedeschia aethiopica*)
Carolina jasmine (yellow jessamine)	*Gelsemium sempervirens*
Castor bean	*Ricinus communis*
Cherry laurel	*Prunus caroliniana*
Chinaberry (bead tree)	*Melia azedarach*
Christmas rose	*Helleborus niger*
Clematis	*Clematis* spp.
Daffodil	*Narcissus* spp.
Deadly nightshade (belladonna)	*Atropoa belladona*
Death cammas (black snakeroot)	*Zigadenus* spp.
Delphinium (larkspur)	*Delphinium* spp.
Dogbane	*Apocynum androsaemifolium*
Dumbcane	*Dieffenbachia* spp.
Elephant ears	*Colocasia antiquorum*
False hellebore	*Veratrum viride*
Four o'clock	*Mirabilis jalapa*
Foxglove	*Digitalis purpurea*
Giant elephant ear	*Alocasia* spp.
Gloriosa lily	*Gloriosa superba*
Golden chain tree (laburnum)	*Laburnum anagryroides*
Goldenseal	*Hydrastis canadensis*

Heavenly bamboo (nandina)	*Nandina domestica*
Henbane (black henbane)	*Hyoscyamus niger*
Horse chestnut (Ohio buckeye)	*Aesculus* spp.
Horse nettle	*Solanum* spp.
Hyacinth	*Hyacinthus orientalis*
Hydrangea	*Hydrangea* spp.
Iris	*Iris* spp.
Ivy (English ivy)	*Hedera* spp.
Jack-in-the-pulpit	*Arisaemia triphyllum*
Jerusalem cherry	*Solanum pseudocapsicum*
Jessamine (jasmine)	*Cestrum* spp.
Jetbead (jetberry)	*Rhodotypos tetrapetala*
Jimson weed	*Datura* spp. (*Brugmansia* spp.)
Jonquil	*Narcissus* spp.
Kentucky coffee tree	*Gymnocladus dioica*
Lantana	*Lantana camara*
Leopard's bane	*Arnica montana*
Lily of the valley	*Convallaria majalis*
Lobelia (cardinal flower, Indian tobacco)	*Lobelia* spp.
Marsh marigold	*Caltha palustris*
May apple (mandrake)	*Podophyllum peltatum*
Mescal bean (Texas mountain laurel, frijo lillo)	*Sophora secundiflora*
Mistletoe	*Phoradendron* spp.
Morning glory	*Ipomoea* spp.
Mountain laurel	*Kalmia latifolia*
Nightshade	*Solanum* spp.
Oleander	*Nerium oleander*
Periwinkle (myrtle, vinca)	*Vinca* spp.
Philodendron	*Philodendron* spp. (*Monstera* spp.)
Pittosporum	*Pittosporum* spp.
Poison hemlock	*Conium maculatum*
Potato	*Solanum tuberosum*
Privet	*Ligustrum* spp.
Rhododendron	*Rhododendron* spp.
Rock poppy (celandyne)	*Chelidonium majus*
Schefflera	*Schefflera* spp.
Spring adonis	*Adonis vernalis*
Spurge	*Euphorbia* spp.
Star of Bethlehem	*Ornithogalum umbellatum*
Sweet pea	*Lathyrus* spp.
Tobacco	*Nicotiana tabacum*
Trumpet flower (chalice vine)	*Solandra* spp.
Water hemlock	*Cicuta maculata*
Wild cherry (black cherry)	*Prunus serotina*
Wisteria	*Wisteria* spp.
Yellow allamanda	*Allamanda cathartica*
Yellow oleander (tiger apple, be still tree, lucky nut)	*Thevetia peruviana*
Yesterday-today-and-tomorrow	*Brunfelsia* spp.

THE ORGANIC EDIBLE FLOWER GARDEN

Toxicity has been discussed at length in the preceding section. However, one aspect of toxicity was saved for this part. Chemicals can become more concentrated in the flower than in the rest of the plant. This is especially true for those that are applied to the plant in the form of fertilizers, or taken in through the roots and leaves. The plant absorbs pesticides, and even herbicides, from the surrounding soil. For that reason, flowers should only be eaten from organic gardens.

Beware of plants purchased in nurseries and garden centers. Flush them well with water. If possible, remove all the soil and replant in the garden or in a container using no chemical additives. I prefer to wait at least a year before eating anything from a nursery-grown plant. However, in the case of annuals, such a wait is impossible. Give them as much time as possible to rid themselves of any toxic material that may have been applied.

Cut flowers are even more dangerous. Consider the fact that the cut-flower industry is thriving in countries where chemicals are not nearly as regulated as they are in the United States. Many of the chemicals that have been outlawed here are now shipped abroad and still used. Once the flowers are cut, they

are put in various chemical solutions to keep them in a salable state as long as possible. As tempting as the flowers from a florist may look, use them to decorate the table only, not the plate.

Excellent books have been written on organic gardening practices. Read one or two if you want more information. This is merely an overview of some of the methods used in organic gardening.

FROM THE BOTTOM UP—THE SOIL

Big, strong, healthy (and delicious) plants grow from healthy soil. Soil is not just dirt. Soil is a living substance with myriad biological, chemical and physical forces constantly at work. It is staggering to think of all that is going on right in the garden, day and night, year after year. Soil is composed of five major elements: air (oxygen, nitrogen, etc.), living organisms (from those too small to see—microscopic bacteria, viruses and fungi—to larger ones—earthworms and insects), humus (organic matter in varying states of decay), water and inorganic matter (particles of minerals and rock).

The culture section in each flower profile gives the best conditions for growing the plant. It is important to learn about the different types of soil, and to know what the soil type is where you want to plant. In one backyard, soil can vary greatly, depending on how it was used and treated in the past. An area that had been a path could have very compacted soil; an area that had been a garden could have a rich, loose loam.

Soil can be sent to a laboratory for a complete analysis, but that is not always necessary. You can determine the basic type of soil you have right in your own garden. Gently squeeze a small amount of moist soil in the palm of your hand. Then rub it between your fingers. Sandy soil feels gritty to the touch. It is made up of the largest particles, and will not hold together when squeezed. Sandy soil is easy to dig in. It drains well—actually almost too well as water draining through it removes most of the nutrients. Silt has a smooth texture, and is made of smaller particles than sandy soil. It can be squeezed, but it does not stay compacted, especially when it is dry. Clay, or heavy soil, is made up of such small particles that it holds its shape when compressed. It feels slick when rubbed between your fingers. That does not allow for air and water movement. Uncompressed, clay can absorb and hold a large amount of water.

The best soil for general gardening is called loam, which is a mixture of the three types just described. When rubbed between the fingers it breaks up into smaller bits. It holds moisture well and encourages the biological activity necessary for happy, healthy soil.

Considering that the soil is the major source of food and water for a plant, it is well worth the effort to create the best possible soil. Good soil should have plenty of organic matter, good drainage and an abundance of nutrients available to the plant. Almost all soil can benefit from the addition of organic matter. Turn the soil with a pitchfork or spade, breaking up any large clods. Add at least ten to fifteen pounds of compost or well-rotted manure and two pounds of rock phosphate (ground up rocks) per hundred square feet. Or simply amend each hole as you plant individual flowers with a couple of handfuls of compost and one-half cup of rock phosphate.

No discussion of soil is complete without talking about pH. pH is a measurement of alkalinity and acidity, ranging from 0 (most acid) to 14 (most alkaline), with 7 as neutral. If the soil pH is not right for a particular plant, it cannot get the nutrients it needs from the soil. There are simple kits for home pH testing. Your local Cooperative Extension Service often offers pH testing for a small fee, as do some nurseries and garden centers. Knowing the pH of the soil, and the requirement of the plant leads to the next step—changing the soil pH. Add elemental sulfur (apply according to package directions) to make the soil more acid, or limestone to make the soil more alkaline (sweet).

MULCH

Mulching with organic material benefits the garden in several ways. Several inches of mulch cuts down on weeds. It conserves water, by cutting down on moisture lost from the soil through evaporation. It keeps the soil temperature more constant. It eventually breaks down, adding humus to the soil, improving soil structure and providing nutrients. As the lower layer of mulch becomes part of the soil, new mulch has to be added, usually once a year. I mulch in the spring, before weeds have established a stronghold. In warmer areas of the country, winter would be the ideal time.

There is a large choice of organic mulching materials. Not all are available in every part of the country. The material used for mulch is a personal choice. Some have a more formal look while others are more natural. Some are free, while others may be pricey for a large area. The choices include grass clippings, straw, cocoa hulls, peanut hulls, pecan

hulls, buckwheat hulls, pine needles, wood chips, wood shavings, sawdust, shredded bark, pine bark nuggets, chopped oak or other leaves, well-rotted manure or ground corn cobs. An addition of nitrogen when mulching helps maintain the carbon-nitrogen ratio of the soil.

COMPOSTING

So much is written about composting that it puts some people off. Composting can be as simple or as complex as you wish. The simplest way to compost is to have two bins. They don't have to be anything fancy, even turkey wire or fencing shaped into a box, thirty-six by thirty-six inches (or round if you prefer). Start out with a couple of inches of soil (the good stuff with all those worms and microorganism). Then add the small weeds you pull up, cuttings from the garden (material no more than one-half inch in diameter; larger items take too long to break down—make a brush pile for these), shredded

leaves (run them over with the lawnmower), grass clippings (no more than one inch at a time as they compact) and all the kitchen garbage except animal products (vegetable peels, leftover cooked vegetables, coffee grounds, egg shells [the exception to the animal rule], the moldy lettuce left in the crisper—you get the idea). Lightly water the pile when first started. After that, if rain does not supply needed moisture, water the pile every week or two. Keep adding to the pile as you accumulate material. It's interesting how there is much less guilt about throwing food out when it's going to the compost pile. It is good to have two bins, because when one becomes filled, you just start adding material to the second. I have found that by the time the second bin is filled, the material in the first has broken down into black gold. No turning, no muss, no fuss.

FERTILIZERS: N-P-K REVEALED

Look at a package of fertilizer and there are three numbers on it, like 5-10-5 or 20-20-20. Those numbers are called the N-P-K ratio, representing the percentage of nitrogen (N), phosphorus (P) and potassium (K) in the fertilizer. What do these elements do for plants?

Nitrogen promotes leaf growth. Phosphorus promotes strong roots, speeds up maturity and is essential for seed and fruit development. Potassium, also called potash, is necessary for cell division in roots and buds.

If it is necessary to amend the soil further, what are the choices for an organic gardener? Nitrogen is readily available in blood meal, cottonseed meal, fish meal and fish emulsion. Activated sewage sludge is also a good source of nitrogen, but it may be high in heavy metals, so avoid it for edibles. Phosphorus is contained in bone meal and rock phosphate. The best sources for potassium are granite dust and ash from hardwoods.

WATERING

Life as we know it cannot exist without water. The most efficient way to water is drip irrigation. Water is released at ground level, right where the roots are. There is minimal water loss through evaporation. An added advantage is that by keeping the leaves dry, some fungal diseases can be avoided. Kits are available to create a customized system, complete with emitters, supply lines, and timers. Systems can be complicated or simple. They are worth the trouble for areas where the soil is not frequently turned and replanted. Another way is to use "leaky pipe" hoses. They are made of a material that water can slowly seep through, delivering water right at ground level near the root zone.

PESTS AND DISEASES

Although no garden is pest-proof, planting a diversity of plants usually results in fewer problems. Try to include one or two plants that persist through the winter (a small tree or shrub, a dwarf evergreen), which may provide a safe haven for praying mantises to deposit their egg cases. Praying mantises eat a prodigious number of aphids, white-flies and garden pests.

A clay pot turned on its side in a shady spot in the garden may attract a toad or frog. They, too, are good guys on the war against insect pests.

It is important, if you have a pest or disease problem, to identify the pest accurately. The local Cooperative Extension Service can be of help—many have telephone hotlines and places to bring plants and pests for identification. Hand pick insects, early in the morning when they are slow to react. If only a small section of a plant is diseased, cut it out and get rid of that portion. (Do not put diseased material on the compost pile.) Dip pruners in alcohol after every cut to avoid spreading disease.

Avoid using any chemical in the garden, even the "organic" ones—they still impact on all the creatures that live in the garden, good and bad. It is best to try and be in harmony with your garden. That is what organic is all about.

GARDEN SCHEMES

Edible flowers are so versatile they can fit into any garden scheme. As you look out into your own garden, you are now able to recognize those flowers that can serve double duty by playing a role in your culinary life.

The following gardens are made up only of edible flowers. They show the duality of the flowers—the gardens are beautiful and can be appreciated even without knowing that all of the flowers are edible.

and one-half feet tall, as there is insufficient room for proper root development.

Grow a single variety (all geraniums, pansies, etc.) or mix flowers for more interest. As the flowers fade, replant the box with fresh plants to keep it going through the seasons.

Window boxes dry out quickly. Check the soil moisture regularly to keep plants from getting stressed.

WINDOW BOX

Any of the smaller plants can be used in window boxes. Never plant anything that will grow more than two to two

CONTAINERS

If space is limited, containers are ideal for growing a few edible flowers. Even if you have a large garden, a container of an often-used edible flower can be handy to have by the kitchen door.

You can grow a whole crop of flowers in containers. Almost any plant can be grown in a container, as long as the container is large enough to support the plant and its root system.

A good rule of thumb is to choose a container that is about twice as large as the spread of the foliage on the plant (when it is fully grown). Do not use galvanized metal with edibles. Otherwise there is no limit on the size and shape of containers except for the space you have to put them. Containers can be small and simple, such as a plastic pot or decorative basket, or large and ornate, such as a terra cotta pot, whiskey barrel or even an old claw foot tub or an unused horse trough.

RAISED BED GARDEN

I was asked to design an edible flower garden in an existing raised bed at a nursery near my home. The semicircular garden is approximately fifteen feet across the back and five feet from front to back. The garden is about three feet high.

More than forty different plants fill the garden—from Rugosa roses providing the backdrop to thyme and oregano spilling down over the stones at the front of the garden. I designed it to change colorfully from spring to summer. By fall, any ragged plants are replaced with chrysanthemums.

I brought some plants from my own garden to put into the raised bed. It was amazing to see how much better they did in the raised bed. With three feet of great, loose, rich soil for the roots to burrow into, the plants needed much less watering than those in my home

garden. An added benefit of working in a raised bed garden is no backache, even after a long day of planting, as there is no bending and back wrenching with a bed three feet off the ground.

THE AUTHOR'S GARDEN

Everything (with the exception of the dwarf Japanese cutleaf maple) that was not edible was ripped mercilessly out of my garden when I began this book project. I designed the garden for interest in all seasons.

With more than sixty different plants (and several varieties of many of them) within a wedge-shaped garden less than twelve feet in radius, there was, and continues to be, a constant battle for space. But this garden continues to grow and evolve, with new plants introduced each season, while reserving enough space to keep old favorites.

Some of my garden gems may be considered weeds to others. A friend volunteered to help weed the garden and to my dismay promptly pulled out all the dandelions I had painstakingly grown from French seeds.

A CALIFORNIA HILLSIDE GARDEN

Carole Saville, garden designer and long-time edible-flower enthusiast, designed her hillside backyard for this book. The garden, in poor soil on a steep terrace, includes more than fifteen different lavenders, as well as other favorites like borage, miniature roses, and Johnny-jump-ups. The plants selected are particularly suited for the drought conditions so prevalent in the West and Southwest. The garden is exquisite from spring through winter, with the lavenders providing interesting form and muted color even when not in bloom.

INDEX